Quicksand
and
Blue Springs

Quicksand and Blue Springs

Exploring the Little Colorado River Gorge

Stephen West Cole

Cover design by Ron Short
Cover photo © Stephen West Cole

Vishnu Temple Press
P O Box 30821
Flagstaff AZ 86003-0821
(928) 556 0742
www.vishnutemplepress.com

to
Sonny Cole

Acknowledgments

While writing this book I was assisted by many people. First, I am grateful to my family members who provided valuable editorial assistance and advice: my wife Sherry, brothers and sisters Sally Mooney, Tom Cole and Wendy Cole, and nephew, Chris Mooney. Hazel Clark's enthusiasm for the project and many hours of indispensible work on the manuscript are also most appreciated. In addition, I wish to thank Boyer Rickel who helped me with the project when it was first taking shape, and especially Paul Morris without whose encouragement and pedagogy the book probably wouldn't have been started. Special thanks go to Dr. Bill Orman for so generously sharing with me his knowledgeof the Gorge and his directions to the Horse Trail. Others who helped me with specific questions were Dick Mathews, Mike Mahany, Ed Stump, Cheryl Soshnik, Ted Page, Tom Martin, Jim Vaaler and Paul Marsh. Last, of course, I thank my most excellent hiking partners, Jeff Cole, Tom Jilek, and Tom Cole.

Contents

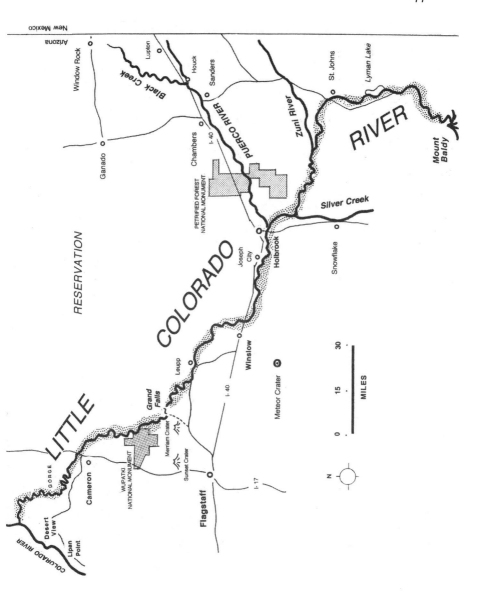

Introduction

In late May of 2001, my brother and I hiked the Little Colorado River Gorge from the town of Cameron, Arizona to its confluence with the Colorado River and out by way of the Beamer and Tanner trails in the Grand Canyon. I found the desert landscape so fascinating that I went back later to explore three remote side canyon routes which enter the chasm. While planning for these trips, I was disappointed to find that little at all had been written about this magnificent wilderness aside from a few articles, some of them dating back to the 1950s, and a smattering of trip reports on the Internet written by backpackers who had done the hike. It is my purpose then to say a few words about the Gorge, to share a few anecdotes, and if the reader will tolerate it, to stray up a few side canyons of memoir. The book is not meant to be a guide, though I hope that anyone exploring the Gorge will find it helpful.

When I first told friends about the book, some of them worried that I might be doing a disservice to the place described herein. They thought that the Little Colorado River Gorge might be better left unrevealed. Drawing attention to it, they reasoned, might serve to popularize it in the same way so many other undiscovered places have been popularized and ruined. After all, the greatest charm of the Gorge is that one can reasonably expect to walk its entire length without seeing a soul. Indeed, some writers faced with this dilemma have gone so far as to misname landmarks or even whole towns in order to confuse their readers as to the exact location of a pristine area.

But the Little Colorado River Gorge has already been discovered and it's such a hassle to hike that only the die-hards ever do it. That fact won't likely be changed much by a book. Only those willing to suffer a long, hard and hazardous trek venture to explore it. I am not kidding. The chafing alone could probably kill you. Such realities pare the number of hikers down to a pretty small number. And the Gorge is protected in other ways. Flooding and impassable mud and quicksand make it impossible to hike a good portion of the year, and travertine dams along the course of the river are not only obstacles for walkers but also discourage all but the most intrepid of kayakers. Even these must wait for the rare occasion when flooding makes conditions suitable for paddling. A hike in the Gorge can also be stopped dead in its tracks by ferocious summer sandstorms which can roar through the canyon for days at a time. Finally, the Gorge is buffered by the Navajo Indian Reservation which tends to filter out the less determined tourists.

Beyond any worries that a book might attract visitors, there is the concern that it might draw someone into danger. A walk into the Gorge could easily become a peripatetic nightmare. Don't let the fact that it has been done entice you into thinking you can do it. Anyone contemplating a visit there should consider the following imperative: Only experienced, extremely fit canyoneers should even think of attempting the Little Colorado River Gorge through-hike. There are numerous dangers, particularly heatstroke in the hotter months. A hiker traveling the Gorge in summer must be adapted physically and, just as importantly, psychologically, to heat stress. Summer flash floods are another threat. This is no joke. Flash flooding in the Gorge has taken the lives of even first-rate canyoneers. The winter months, of course, offer their own hazard in the form of hypothermia. Drowning, snakebite, and especially falling, comprise just a few of the many year-round possibilities, and looming always is the ever-present reality that emergency help might not arrive for days if at all. That said, the Little Colorado River Gorge still offers a truly unique adventure to experienced canyoneers. To them I wish a safe and happy hike.

1
Little Colorado

The Little Colorado River Gorge is one of the biggest, longest, most remote, canyon wildernesses left on the continent and, if you're a desert canyon lover, perhaps the most alluring and beautiful. It is a narrow, serpentine chasm cut deeply into the Colorado Plateau, spirited with gushing blue springs, travertine terraces, turquoise pools and plunging canyon walls. It is also cursed with quicksand, razed by scouring flash floods, isolated from the world and in the summer roasting hot. In places the walls are so steep you could throw a stone all the way to the riverbed a half mile below. I could find no record of anyone hiking through it before 1964.

A hiker disappearing into the Gorge has stepped out of time. Not until you reach the Colorado River in the Grand Canyon nearly sixty miles away, can you expect to see another human being. From the confluence you still face a hard, lonely trek out along the hazardous Beamer Trail and up the challenging Tanner before reaching blacktop.

The Gorge's most appealing aspect is simple. There isn't anybody there. Even the Navajos, through whose reservation the river flows, have little reason to visit the gorge of what Colorado River runners call the Little C or the LCR. The Hopis sometimes walk in part of the way to visit their sacred salt mines just downstream of the confluence, and a few miles into the lower end of the Gorge where they worship at a holy spring called the Sipapu. But aside from that, there isn't much traffic. No cities lie along the river's course through the Gorge, no houses or farms or settlements. No roads lead into it. There are no bandits or contrabanistas, no mountain bikers, no policemen, no rangers or cowboys. There isn't anybody down there.

The sanest way into the Gorge is at the town of Cameron between Flagstaff and Tuba City. Any other entrance that might cut the trip shorter is a royal headache. The primitive Horse Trail, which allegedly enters at mile thirty-five (measured from the bridge at Cameron), requires a confusing drive across back roads on the Res even if you know where the hell you're going. The Blue Spring trail is even more trouble. It enters at mile forty-two, but you also have an even harder time finding it, and the descent is dangerous, with plenty of places to make a richly-prolonged, straight air plunge. The Salt Trail, which the Hopis still use on their pilgrimages, offers an adequate entrance to the Gorge. Coming in and exiting on the Salt Trail, a hiker could avoid the 20 miles of rugged hiking out via the Beamer and Tanner trails in the Grand Canyon. But like the others, locating it is like running down a rumor, and in order to see the best attractions like Blue Spring at mile 42, you'd have to slog miles and miles upcanyon anyway. I decided the best route was the most obvious, the simplest, the one that takes in the whole Gorge from Cameron to the confluence and exits via Beamer and Tanner. Counting the twists and turns, I guessed it on the lean side of eighty miles.

There aren't many people who can give advice on the LCR Gorge trek. I was fortunate, however, to acquire reliable, first-hand input on this wilderness route from a person who had done it. He was a bedraggled, dispirited hiker I spoke to on the Tanner Trail one scalding June morning. He was just an hour from the Grand Canyon's South Rim and the end of the journey. My brother and I were just starting an ill-advised hot weather descent to the river. His advice on hiking the Gorge from Cameron to the Colorado River and out? A laconic, emphatic, "Don't."

In any backpacking trip, there is always the problem of getting someone interested in coming with you. Not many people share such enthusiasms, particularly when they involve trudging through 42 miles of triple digit temperatures, and drinking out of mudholes just to get to the hard part. I was willing to walk the Gorge alone. There is, nevertheless, nothing wrong with caution. Even with a companion, the area is so inaccessible that in the event of an emergency it might take days for someone to hike out for help. I knew of only one person who was likely to accompany me. But my brother Jeff is sometimes difficult to locate. You can call his home at noon or 4 a.m. and he will not be there. I don't know where he is, but he sure isn't at home. For years at a time, he has disappeared into South America and no one hears much from him. I was lucky this time. I was able to reach him by phone and email as well, but when I casually broached the subject of hiking the Little Colorado River Gorge, he brushed the idea aside. "Naw, I gotta work the end of May." I put the subject to him a couple more times and he still showed not the remotest interest. "Naw. I gotta work the end of May."

Weeks passed. At the end of April I tried a different approach:

Jeff: Thought I'd email you and let you know that everything is still GO for our Little Colorado River Gorge Expedition. Don't worry about the permits. They're all bought and paid for (both Navajo Nation Permits and Grand Canyon) so don't even give that a thought. I've also got all the gear: packs, stoves trekking poles, tarps, food—everything ready to go. The itinerary is May 26th with an exit out via Beamer and Tanner in the Grand Canyon on June 5th. Let me know if there are any last minute changes you'd like to make, though this late in our plans they'll have to be damn small ones as everything is pretty-well finalized. You'll have to fly out here on the 25th or sooner in order for us to get to Cameron and begin the trek. What a relief that this is finally a done deal and that you are on board and that everything is A-okay and full speed ahead.

Jeff called shortly asking if there was anything special he needed to bring.

"We've been all through that," I said.

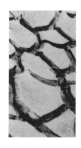

2
Twice Told Trail
June 4, 1996

Perhaps it would be all right to begin at the end. The Tanner Trail is the last leg and exit route for the Little Colorado River Gorge trek. Trekking the Tanner is difficult enough in and of itself without facing it for the first time at the end of a seventy-odd-mile hike. Anyone attempting the Gorge would be wise to know the Tanner and understand it a little. Fortunately, I had done it twice, once years ago with Jeff and another time solo. The first hike went poorly. My brother and I had foolishly tackled the Tanner one scorching June day in 1996 encumbered by a combined load of eighteen quarts of water. It was on that trip that we met the unhappy Gorge hiker. He and a younger companion were just an hour from the rim. We had caught them at the wrong end of their hike. They were not buoyed with enthusiasm like us. They were morose, unfriendly. Maybe it wasn't the trail itself. Perhaps they were just sick of each other, but it was clear that the experience had taken a toll.

The younger one was dressed only in his underpants, dirty white briefs, and all down his legs were deep, dark red, painful-looking scratches which spoke of some disastrous fall through a thorny tree. They were not in the mood to discuss any particulars of the Little Colorado River Gorge. My assurance that the trailhead was only an hour away didn't cheer them at all. They trudged slowly away dragging their shadows behind them like black sledges.

The Tanner Trail, though unmaintained, is nevertheless a well-defined one. You would have to be an idiot to get lost on it. In fact, losing the Tanner Trail, I would guess, is pretty darn near impossible even for first time hikers. It took Jeff and me less than an hour to do it. Not long after we left the two Gorgemen, my brother stopped short. "What's the matter?"

"The trail."

"What?"

"It was here a minute ago."

Already the dialogue, bred of familiarity, took its customary shape.

"Goddamnit. Move aside. Lemme look. Well, it does seem a little vague here. Must be just a thin stretch is all."

We found ourselves following animal trails down a steep, rocky canyon and wound up in places where any slip was death.

"Jesus," I said. "Let's go back up. You wandered us off the trail somewhere up there."

"Back up? All the way back up there? Like Hell. I'm cutting up this talus. It'll likely cross the main trail."

Now it happens that on any hiking permit issued for treks into the Grand Canyon, there is a space requiring the name of the trip leader. Since I applied for the permit, I was christened with this lofty appellation and I had taken the heady title to heart. It was time to take charge, assert my authority.

"Listen, you," I said evenly. "The only sane thing is to backtrack even if it does mean a hard climb. You want to get lost out here and have the rangers find us all bloated up like a couple of dead cows with horseflies all over us? Now be smart and follow me." I turned and started back but he grabbed my elbow.

"Look," he said. "The trail has only one way it can go. It's gotta be right up over this talus and to the left. You don't really want to climb back up, do you?"

I looked up the steep canyon. "Well, I'm inclined to agree with you," I said.

We began a dangerous scramble over a huge hill of loose talus and, having summited, found another even steeper hill to climb. All the while the mercury was rising. Up out of the brushy side canyon, there wasn't a sliver of shade and the sun was roasting us alive.

"Damn, this pack is heavy. I almost fell over backwards a minute ago. Maybe we ought to dump some water."

"Don't give me that," I said. "I'm carrying a half gallon of your water already. I've got eleven quarts breaking my back. Don't tell me about heavy."

"I'm fryin' here."

"Well, if you'd listened to me in the first place we'd already be back on the trail. Now you don't know where the hell you are, do you?"

"Oh, yeah. Like you know where we are."

"Oh, I'll tell you where we are. We're lost. That's where we are!"

The conversation, packed with equally erudite witticisms, continued until we reached, exhausted, the Tanner Trail which suddenly appeared before us like a six lane highway. We slumped down in the shade of a boulder in a sober mood.

"Well," my brother said finally, "that was a screw up. We won't do that again."

"No, we won't," I agreed.

For the walk out we cached a gallon of water at the Stegosaur, a jagged rock formation near the bottom of the switchbacks, and another at the top of the Redwall, a massive 600-foot canyon-encircling cliff of limestone. We were not being overly cautious. Nine quarts apiece is the recommended supply for a summer descent. Dying of thirst on the Tanner Trail has been done plenty of times.

Below the Redwall we traveled across what in my notebook I called, "Hills of colossal dimensions falling away." The wind started up and quickly became ferocious. It blew needle-sharp sheets of sand and threatened to send us off the trail and down the steep hills. In addition to this, my feet were killing me. The steep descent and heavy load had banged them up. Each of ten thousand steps whacked my feet on rocks. I had no blisters but the soft-soled shoes I was wearing offered scant protection and left me footsore and limping.

Lower, in the Dox Formation, the wind was fiery hot. One hundred and ten degrees. Years of cross country races and marathons had left my brother heat-resistant but even my practice hikes up Pima Canyon in Phoenix had not prepared me for this kind of heat. There was no way to get away from the sun and it was baking my brain. The section of the canyon below us is nicknamed Furnace Flats. Occasionally, when the effort of walking built up too much fire, I stopped in the trail to compose myself.

Hours later, the bottom of the canyon appeared and we crunched across the gravel of Tanner Wash. At the river, we slumped down in the shade of the trees. Then we limped to the bank and iced our feet in the clear, green water. There were only two people at the river. The first told us he was from Flagstaff and made postcards of the canyon for a living. He seemed quite at home at Tanner; his clothes were clean and he looked as if he had hardly broken a sweat getting here. I didn't talk to him long, but I had the impression that he had not come in via Tanner but by some other route, maybe Beamer, and that he had been in the canyon a while. The other was a brown-skinned, bearded Californian who had been hiking for a month. He told us that he had finagled another twenty days on his hiking permit. "It was either that or work," he said. The choice had been simple. The permits were free. The next year the park would adopt a new twenty-dollar, plus-four-dollar-a-night non-refundable price tag for canyon trekking. It would, they said, help revenues and protect the park. The ragged Californian was slow and peaceful in his speech and manner. He was barefoot and both big toe-nails were the color of plums.

"That happened on the Escalante Route," he said. "The downhill walking is what does it."

That night we slept on the deep sand at the mouth of Tanner Canyon. I'd brought no sleeping bag. It wouldn't drop much under 90 degrees all night. Instead, I was wrapped in a sheet which I brought only to keep the bugs off.

Tanner Canyon was originally a Hopi route and it was near the head of Tanner, Lipan Point, that the first Europeans supposedly saw the Grand Canyon. About fifty years before Shakespeare started writing his plays, a Spaniard named Garcia Lopez de Cardenas looked over the rim. The distances he beheld cozened his mind. He perceived the river a mile below as nothing more than a small stream in a big gully. He ordered three of his men to descend to it, but the reality of the scene soon became apparent. He later wrote not so eloquently, "What at first seemed easy turned out to be very difficult and hard." Cardenas soon abandoned the attempt to reach the Colorado River and went on to plunder elsewhere.

Tanner was, as local folklore asserts, a route for horse thieves in the early part of the twentieth century. The outlaws, it is said, stole their horses in Utah, changed their brands and after driving them across the river moved them out via Tanner and on to Flagstaff for sale. The process was then reversed. The rustlers stole a new batch of horses in Flagstaff and herded them back the same way to Utah.

The stars were bright and I fell asleep to the soothing white sound of Tanner rapids. Before sunrise I got up, boiled coffee and cooked freeze-dried lasagna on my tiny gas stove. Jeff limped over from his bed in the sand and we discussed our predicament in the dark.

"Let's face it. We're a mess," I said. "Trail beat us up pretty bad. It might take us two days to get out of here. How're your feet?"

He showed me a patchwork of moleskins he'd applied during our breaks the day before. Then he showed me his boots. He'd taken a knife and slashed them along the sides.

"That should relieve some of the pressure," he said.

They weren't even his boots. They were a gift from a buddy and they didn't fit.

"I've got to discard some weight." I told him. "All that trail mix and other food. I haven't got the stomach to eat even half of it. I bet that California guy'd take it. He looks half starved."

"I already asked him yesterday. He said not to be rude, but he didn't want it. Said he was perfectly happy. Says he doesn't eat much – he's got lentils and dried fish."

"Funny," I said. "Dried fish sounds kind of good for down here. That guy knows what he's doing. We could probably learn something from him. Those M & M's I packed make me sick even thinking about them."

The sky was lightening and the river turning the color of shale as we headed back up the canyon. We had to leave Furnace Flats before it caught fire. We carried a gallon of water each. Once, a pain in my back stopped me. I downed a handful of anti-inflammatories and continued up what I would later call Four-Motrin Hill.

By nine o'clock we had beaten the Redwall and shortly thereafter reached our cache point. Up in the junipers it was almost cool. Somewhere near the Stegosaur we made a hot lunch of turkey tetrazzini and espresso coffee. Jeff picked a handful of Mormon tea, also called ephedra, and boiled it up. It wasn't bad. You could develop a taste for it. Preparing it is easy. You can simply boil the stalks, which look like tiny sticks of green bamboo. Splitting them first reveals a bronze-colored core and makes for a stronger brew. The ubiquitous ephedra grows in abundance from the Colorado Plateau through the Sonoran Desert all the way to the salty dunes edging the Sea of Cortez.

We camped at the bottom of the last switchbacks, too beat to brave the last ascent. I climbed up to examine a little cave in the rocks nearby and was surprised to find a cardboard box jammed inside. In the cache were packages of AA batteries, cans of tuna fish, candles, a mess kit, and some aluminum pouches of freeze-dried food. There were also six empty cans with triangular holes punched by a church key—presumably improvised lanterns for the candles, though I couldn't imagine how anyone could need more than one. The rat-eaten litter was all that was left of someone's canyon dream.

The box also contained a copy of *On Foot in the Grand Canyon* by Sharon Spangler. A sales slip inside revealed that it had been purchased the previous spring in San Diego. I'd checked the same book out of the library before I came. I considered packing this junk out of the canyon as a public service, but I couldn't face it. I took only the abandoned book which I judged worth the extra effort to lug out. In the book Spangler describes her adventures on the South Rim trails and the engaging, enthusiastic personal accounts of her canyon treks serve the hiker new to the canyon better than an ordinary, dispassionate guide book. Much of the book describes trips with her husband Bob whose help in preparing and editing the manuscript she mentions in her acknowledgments. But there was more to the story of Robert Merlin Spangler than his wife knew.

Perhaps it could begin at 11:24 a.m. on April 11, 1993 as Bob Spangler stood patiently in line with hikers waiting for permits at the Backcountry Office on the South Rim. When it came his turn he stepped to the counter and said, "Yes, please, can you help me? My wife has fallen off the Redwall on Horseshoe Mesa. She fell to her death." He was referring to his new and third wife, Donna. He and Sharon were at this time divorced. The rangers listened with horror as Spangler told them how his wife had fallen 160 feet off a cliff near Grandview Point as she had posed for a photo. Rangers found her body where he had left it draped with a blue tarp, her face underneath covered lovingly with a red bandanna.

Four years earlier Spangler, then divorced from Sharon, had met Donna, a Littleton, Colorado aerobics instructor with five children from a previous marriage. The marriage lasted a year before tensions began to grow. The two were not well matched as they held different interests. For one thing, Donna Spangler, unlike his previous wife, did not share her husband's enthusiasm for hiking. Still, in April of 1993 the couple scheduled a trip down the Grandview Trail. Below Horseshoe Mesa they turned onto the rugged Page Spring Trail and camped that evening at Hance Creek. The next day they hiked back up Page Spring and camped again. It was the following morning as they reached the last big drop-off on their way out the Grandview Trail that Robert Spangler, according to his own later testimony, resolved to solve his marital troubles once and for all. It was now or never, he thought. No cliffs above this point could assure a fatal plunge. There was a brief face-to-face struggle. A small woman, Donna Spangler was no match for her powerful husband. He shoved her off. Then he climbed down and washed her face, covered her and headed to the Backcountry Office.

It would seem that such a story could not get worse, but the heinous act of pushing his third wife off a cliff was exceeded by the unspeakable nature of an earlier crime. In December of 1978, unhappy with his first wife, Nancy, and then enamored with a blameless Sharon Cooper, Robert made plans he felt would be more convenient than divorce. Prior to his crime, Spangler typed out a suicide note that he tricked Nancy into signing, saying it was a Christmas letter. The subsequent killing included both his teenaged daughter and son. Incredibly, the note and a flimsy alibi did the trick. Though suspicious, the police wrote it off as a murder-suicide and

Spangler was not charged in the triple slaying. Nor was he charged in the death of his third wife at Grandview Point. It was only in 1993 when he arrived at a Colorado hospital with his dying ex-wife, the author, Sharon, who he claimed had taken an overdose of drugs, that investigators took action. They accused him of causing all five deaths. He promptly confessed to the first four murders but not to Sharon's, complaining, "You're giving me credit for one I'm not guilty of." Incredibly, the police became convinced that Sharon Spangler's death was after all a suicide.

As incomprehensible and tragic as Sharon Spangler's story is, it should be noted, in this cynical age, that she was guilty of nothing other than bad luck. Her book, still in print, continues to introduce hikers to the Canyon.

Sleeping up in the junipers near the rim, I found the sheet inadequate. This was no Furnace Flats. The temperature fell enough to make me shiver all night. It was a relief to start climbing when the morning finally came. Two hours to the top. We discarded our excess water and started up the trail. The Tanner had whupped us pretty bad. We walked on trembling legs, footsore, aching, entirely exhausted from the experience, gladdened only by the knowledge that hiking the trail twice was so easily avoidable.

3

The Solo Hikers
June 5, 2000

Four whole years passed before I walked Tanner again. Since it was the last leg of the Gorge hike, I thought I'd take another look at it. The second hike down Tanner went better. I had learned that walking in full sun, overloading your pack and rushing things can make for misery. By now I had also learned the value of trekking poles for both descending and ascending a steep trail like Tanner. I would be starting the trail late in the morning but this time I prudently planned to camp above the Redwall and walk the second half of the trail early the next day.

It was ten o'clock before I reached Lipan Point where I parked my rented Hyundai, hefted the pack and descended through the dusty switchbacks where the Tanner snaked down steeply through the pines. This time I did not stray from the clear and well-trodden path, but I had another kind of trouble. More than halfway down the first switchbacks, I realized that I had left my hiking permit in the car. Damn! I began to trudge back up. I had taken ten uphill steps before my brain, like some great derelict ship, fired off a broadside synapse and I thought to dump the pack. I strode up the trail.

Half an hour later another belated salvo upstairs informed me that the car key was in the pack! Back down the trail. There was lots of time for my exasperation to build. By the time I retrieved the key, I was furious. I cursed it and spat on it, made ugly allusions to its parentage, nothing any errant key hasn't heard. At the car I snatched the permit off the front seat, stuffed it in my pocket, and marched off like a miffed hairdresser.

It was pushing noon by the time I reached the pack again. Time to attach that tag before I forgot. I stuck my hand in my pocket. Nothing there. I stood blinking. I turned around a couple of times, first one direction then the other, the way dogs do before they lie down. I must have dropped it up there somewhere. I sat down in the trail. I didn't weep much, but some. A pinyon jay squawked cheerfully in a low bough and I gave a halfhearted glance at a nearby stone. My emotions now were tempered by a kind of resignation and after a few whimpers, I rose and ascended the trail once more, too dispirited even to swear. Fortune relented a little and I found the tag barely ten minutes uphill where it lay in the middle of the path. I picked it up and turned it over in my hands, half expecting *Hello, Stupid* to be printed on it.

There is nothing that can be done about such things and they occur over and over, and the challenge of overcoming and correcting small mistakes or unforeseen difficulties born of stupidity or absentmindedness is part of the game. Sometimes a large part. And if you're not careful, a series of innocuous screwups can add up to disaster. Just past the foot of the switchbacks stood an imposing red metal stop sign mounted on a steel post. It read:

STOP. HEAT KILLS.

Smaller print on the sign went on to emphasize the danger of death by heatstroke and advised hikers not to proceed unless they began their hike before seven a.m. or after four p.m. Under no circumstances, the sign, implored, should one attempt to walk to the river and back in one day. I was a little offended by this intrusive city road sign in the wilderness but I was soon beyond it and skirting Cardenas and Escalante buttes past oddly familiar places. I took my time.

Alongside the trail, swaying Utah agaves grew from the rocks, their long, flowering fronds alive with bumble bees. I reached a place atop the Redwall where a gnarled juniper log was poised like a bristling gray sea lion with points here and there handy for hanging gear. I leaned the pack against it and set up my exceedingly simple camp. It was late afternoon and the air in the canyon uncertain. A hummingbird rocketed past like something fired from a sling shot. I munched from a giant bag of oily, homemade Teriyaki jerky, gritty with salt, and later as the light faded, I set up my midget stove, for I am always happiest when boiling water for tea or coffee or chocolate. It was very peaceful and remote there above the Redwall, but even Tanner in summer is not a place where solitude is guaranteed. There are a lot of people in the Grand Canyon and they come from all over the world. It was almost dark when I heard the crunch of Vibram soles. He marched by sporting a Power Bar T shirt and a brand new, gray, internal frame Gregory pack. Soon it was dark and the sky full of stars and I was alone again and sound asleep.

I packed out early. The rough section of trail dropped over the Redwall and I followed it carefully, watching for loose stones and patches of scree. The trail was cool and the canyon very quiet. The light was subdued in a way that made everything seem somber and timeless and lonely. But as I traversed the colossal hills leading to Tanner Beach, the sun spilled over the cliffs, the endorphins rose, sweat broke, and I was filled with a giddy sense of anticipation.

I had by now put the little distant thumb of Desert View Watch Tower, perched high on the rim, far behind me. The smooth, red side of the enormous hill fell away like a sigh. Soon I reached the rocky bottom of Tanner Wash, which I followed right to the river. The beach I remembered at the foot of the drainage had changed. When my brother and I had hiked it before, the beach was bigger. Now it was encroached upon by river stones, reduced by the fluctuating water level to less than half its previous size.

Just upstream was a little copse of tamarisk and downstream a smaller tangle of "tammies." I shed the pack under the upstream trees and whacked my walking stick around the branches here and there. This was a prime location for what I once heard someone refer to as terrorist squirrels, who chew nasty holes in your pack if you let your guard down for even a second. I scared up only a couple of tiny black-tailed gnatcatchers who flickered away.

I spent the balance of the day hiking out to Cardenas

Creek and exploring the broad flood plains of rock and sand and desert broom, and stepping across big, round river stones and ancient gray logs, feeling the heat radiating off silt and stone and the damp cold breath of the river on my face and the texture of the canyon, its pebbles, its silt, through my Vibram soles. The sand and the rock and the Colorado's water, an emerald green, blazed in the bright sunlight. There was almost always a light breeze keeping the heat at bay. Once, though, as I trudged along a trail of white-hot, puffy silt, the wind gave up and the heat clamped down. My temperature topped out, and I was forced to lie very still in the tamarisk shadows with the signs of approaching heat stroke as clear and unmistakable as the sharp resinous scent of salt cedar rising around me. I lay there for a long time until the fire seemed to spill off my face and a breeze rose and walked away with it.

As I wandered, I recalled the story of Bert Loper, a well-known early river pioneer often referred to in boatman literature as the Old Man of the Canyon. In 1944 the 79-year-old Loper suffered a heart attack while operating his cataract boat near 24 ½ Mile Rapid. He was seen to fall overboard and drift silently away in the muddy current. That was the last anyone saw of him.

Thirty-five years later, some human bones were uncovered in the sandy alluvium near Cardenas Creek, some fifty miles downstream from the place where Loper fell in. The skull showed the characteristics of an elderly person. Could these bones be the remains of Bert Loper? The skull was "fleshed out" by a sketch artist adept in anthropometry, a skill the police often utilize in attempting to identify a person from his bones. It sure looked like Bert. The remains were interred in a family plot in a Salt Lake City cemetery.

But the story of Bert Loper is perhaps not yet closed after all. In 1976, an acquaintance of mine, exploring the canyon near Cardenas Creek and having heard of the discovery of Loper's skeleton, decided to do a little bone prospecting himself. He poked around in the sand with a stick. To his astonishment, he immediately unearthed more human bones. He was a young and carefree man who didn't think to report the find and he left the bones where they were. But his story raises a question: if Loper's remains had been removed, whose bones could these have been? I had assumed that they were simply overlooked leftovers from a less-than-thorough excavation of Bert Loper until I met author and river runner Tom Martin, who advanced another theory, one which might make more sense.

In 1956, a fiery aircraft collision strewed the wreckage of two huge airliners on both sides of the river near the mouth of the Gorge, a scant fifteen miles upstream from Cardenas Creek. There is little doubt that passengers rained down upon the canyon and that some of them splashed into the river. Martin hypothesized that the bones discovered at Cardenas Creek more likely came from this nearby crash than from Loper's boat, a whopping fifty miles upstream. The identification done on the "Loper" skull was, all told, a subjective one (DNA testing was, of course, not available at the time) and it makes sense that any human bones found at Cardenas are more likely those from victims of the more recent and local tragedy right upstream. After all, why would a hiker still be uncovering remains there after "Bert's" removal?

Back under the trees at the little beach, I met two men, both older than I. One was very lean and spoke with a vaguely German accent; the other was a New Englander with a full head of white hair and an old Gerry pack. We sat comfortably on the sand in the late afternoon shade and talked. The lean one had just returned from a day hike out to the Little Colorado River via the Beamer trail, almost a twenty-mile jaunt and the penultimate stretch of the Little C Gorge walk. The New Englander was on the first leg of a ten-day trip along the ill-defined Escalante Route. He would eventually exit on the Bright Angel Trail. He was from New Hampshire and had planned to hike with his son. The father and son adventure was derailed by the son's acquisition of a new girlfriend and the father had come alone. He told us that he came to the canyon once a year to make a ten-day hike. We were all three solo hikers, and as we talked it became apparent that we were the same breed of cat.

"Remember that part in *The Man Who Walked Through Time* when he threw the wine bottle in the river?" he asked. It didn't occur to him that either of us had might not have read Colin Fletcher's book. We talked of Edward Abbey and Powell's Journal, and the stories of hiking guru, NAU math professor Harvey Butchart, sometimes called the Obi-Wan Kenobi of Grand Canyoneering. It was Dr. Butchart who first described the Gorge after hiking upstream from the foot of the Horse Trail to Cameron in 1964. "I know Harvey," said the lean one, and filled us in on the whereabouts and recent doings of this legend. "He's in his nineties now."

"I heard that," I said.

Butchart's friend worked as a boatman during the river season and told of the Beamer trail I was interested in. I already had him pegged as an expert canyoneer. He didn't seem to think the twenty-odd-mile round trip to the Little C and back was much.

"I hear it's got some scary stretches where the wind, if it's bad, will blow you off the edge," I said.

"No. There's a long walk through the sand though, and that's tiring." He went on to say that he had seen a dead Colorado River squawfish up near the confluence. His identification was probably off. Most of the native piscean fauna including these huge river minnows have been extirpated by the plunging water temperature brought about by Glen Canyon Dam. The warmer and often muddy Little Colorado River, however, preserves a semblance of the original habitat and a remnant population of endangered humpback chub has held on, and it is likely that the fish he observed was of this odd-looking species.

As we talked, a flock of grackles stormed in from over the river and up under the trees where my pack lay propped against a stump. The big birds began casing it like squirrels. As stately as roosters, they hopped and nodded and argued. I was surprised to see grackles here. The great-tailed grackle was wholly absent from the Southwest until the late sixties when they began for whatever reason to make their move north from Mexico. Phoenix and its surrounding cities were soon inundated with them, and their varied whistles and musical notes, once so exotic, became familiar urban voices. Now they were working over some spilled oatmeal next to my pack. I wondered if they might tear through the fabric like squirrels. A hiker I met once on the trail told me that the canyon's trenchant ravens had learned to unzip a backpack, pocket by pocket, and dine buffet style.

After a while, we sauntered off each our own way. I wandered over to my pack and tipping it forward, discovered a small pile of finely shredded green nylon and a ragged mouse hole in the back. I hadn't been twenty feet away and a terrorist squirrel had gotten me. I'd been concentrating on the grackles. I unpacked the bottom compartment and found the squirrel had missed the mark. Guided by his sensitive, selective nose, his aim had been perfect. The hole was lined up precisely with my stash of mixed nuts, but he'd been foiled by the impenetrable aluminum cooking pot enclosing the sack. I grieved a little over the injured pack. How to fix it? Duct tape, of course, that indispensable backpacking item. Two square swaths across each side of the hole patched it good as new.

That night I camped at the little spit of white sand at the edge of the river where Jeff and I had camped four years before. I boiled water on my midget stove and mixed in stroganoff noodles. While these soaked, I sautéed a few handfuls of dried mushrooms in an improvised *au jus* made of water and the contents of a Top Ramen beef flavor package. Then I stirred it all together and ate the mixture with chopsticks, sitting on a poncho in the dusk. It was very peaceful with the rushing sound of the rapids and the cool smell of the river and, as night came, a familiar, silent mood enveloped the canyon. I lay on my sleeping bag and watched the sky where meteors streaked thinly like little spasms of fear, and satellites crossed with a mathematical precision which made them seem as cold and indifferent as stars.

Three a.m. People were walking by, their voices soft in the night, their flashlights flickering eerily. The trail led them quite near me and I was vaguely aware that they were stepping lightly to avoid waking me. They passed twice having taken a wrong turn, and then headed up Tanner Wash. They were rushing to beat the sun. An hour later I got up and made coffee. I took my time, listened to the river. Finally, I rolled up my sleeping bag, repacked my stuff and tidied up the camp before shouldering the pack. It was still dark, but just barely. The five quarts of water I lugged was probably more than I needed. Cached atop the Redwall was a half gallon extra and farther up the trail at the Stegosaur another.

Far up the hills, I looked casually back from where I'd come, to a colossal vista of hills, temples and buttes, and a green meandering river, and as the sun lightened the canyon, I saw far below a small black dot, like an ant moving up the trail. He was far away, but gaining fast.

It was Butchart's friend, a real flyer. Soon he was next to me. "Woke up and saw you were gone. Figured I better get moving too." He planned to top out that morning. I was taking my time. I'd camp at the bottom of the last switchbacks. We talked a while and compared equipment a little. He had a Jansport pack.

Time to get walking again. He made a grandiloquent gesture, a sweeping of the hand as if to say, "After you, my dear Alphonse."

"No way. You'll run right over me." I was right. He flew easily ahead and disappeared up the Redwall. I never saw him again.

I retrieved my half gallon cache atop the Redwall and wandered along until I reached the juniper sea lion. The sun was high and blazing now. I stopped in the shade of a living juniper and assessed my water situation. Way ahead. Almost a gallon all together not counting the half gallon at the Stegosaur. Still too hot to hike. I lay back in the shadows and fell asleep.

When I awoke, the sun was getting ready to drop behind the cliffs, and when it did, I contoured the long, curving Tanner in the red shade of Cardenas and Escalante Buttes until I reached the next cache point. I had chosen several landmarks to lead me up a hill to where the water was hidden behind a jumble of boulders: a small cluster of purple asters, an oddly shaped rock and an old twisted juniper. A small kingsnake banded with black and yellow glided under the rocks and disappeared in the cool darkness between them.

I camped where my brother and I had on our first hot weather trek, just at the bottom of the switchbacks in a little clearing enclosed by brush and boulders and trees. A big spiny lizard approached and did threatening pushups, to show me how mad I made him. Before light the next morning I discarded all but a quart of my water and upon reaching the trailhead a couple of hours later, I knew I had Tanner figured out. My first hike had left me with an exaggerated perspective of Tanner's difficulties. The trick to Tanner was patience, shade and water. It would be an easy hike out at the end of the Little Colorado Gorge Expedition. The only thing left was to do it.

4

Little Colorado Day One
Cottonwood Camp
May 26, 2001

Our trip into the Gorge starts with an exaltation of cedar waxwings over our heads at the Cameron Bridge. The channel is wide here and simple to get into but muddier than I had hoped. There was a splattering of rain a week ago and I'm worried that there will be quicksand blocking our way in this first stretch. It's wet, but we get through by winding along the edges of yellow pools and mudholes and stepping through sloppy spots when they seem shallow enough. We slog across broad passes of mud covering a base of clay hardpan. It's like walking over concrete that's covered with four inches of green Cool Whip. Exiting such expanses of muck, I stagger in weighted shoes like Frankenstein's monster.

The Gorge is at first just a wide wash and we crunch over pentagons of cracked clay, and mush through expanses of red mud. There is a multiformity of surfaces. Often we cross stretches of cracked, red clay as brittle as pot shards. Then big green plates, hard on the top, wet on the bottom, which often slough loose and slip under our feet. In places the mud has split and curled in the hot sun like paper fringe, creating lacy mud flowers with smooth, clean river stone centers.

If Eskimos have many words to describe varieties of snow, surely the native travelers of this gorge had words to describe the different forms of mud cracks. Already we are naming them. We walk across crispies, crunchies, crackers, snappers and occasional stretches of platters that break like inch-thick pale-green china under our Vibram soles, occasionally giving us a painful whack on the back of the ankle as they snap in two. Our Rabelaisian nomenclature for mud is perhaps best left unrecorded.

Three miles down the wash, Jeff has his first blister. A big one on the heel. He peels down his sock revealing a red, shiny layer of exposed skin screaming with angry nerve ends and a flap hanging down like a toilet seat. It kind of snuck up on him, he says. Seventy-seven miles to go.

Already it feels like wilderness. No one is here. The broad path is edged with cottonwoods. The sun is low in the sky, blinding hot in our faces. We pass under power lines which are singing like cicadas over the wash and we continue walking almost until dark. We make barely five miles but it's late and we are tired. There is a gentle but steady wind. We set our packs up under a big roaring cottonwood on the left bank.

I christen the place Cottonwood Camp, though I might well have called it Camp Gophersnake for as we leaned back on our packs, an impressive specimen slithered past our feet. It was a very long snake, five feet at least, sliding up the hill of sand and into the brush.

The Sonoran Gophersnake, often called a bullsnake, is among the largest snakes in Arizona and the most common in the southern Grand Canyon tributaries. It's a powerfully built reptile reported to reach an astonishing length of eight feet. It kills its prey by constriction. When antagonized, it will vibrate its tail to imitate a rattler, lunge, hiss and spit at an intruder. But it is easily tamed, and because it can be safely handled, it is chosen by the Hopis for their snake ceremonies. It might be noted that nothing in this world is exaggerated more than the length of a snake, unless it be the size of a Minnesota walleye. The reader will appreciate then, that I have modified my original six-foot assessment of this gophersnake by nearly 17 percent. And while we are being honest, the heat is also bearable, barely 100 degrees, and the dry wind is cooling.

We do a bird survey from Cottonwood Camp and spot a Say's phoebe, several kingbirds and a Lazuli bunting colored like a blue parakeet. Our appetites have shut down, not uncommon the first night out, but we still want our hot chocolate. I fire up my homemade Camp Dragon wood-burning stove and stoke it with some finger-sized sticks. Jeff is impressed. "God, it just roars."

"Not only that," I brag, "but it weighs half what a Zip Stove does—eight ounces—and has a more secure base. I slip a couple more fat twigs under the pot and turn the tiny battery-powered fan to full power. A circle of flames jets up around the pot. "Packs smaller too. Boils a quart of water in four minutes."

Here at Cottonwood Camp we put the Camp Dragon through its first field test. We pop more sticks into the cylinder where they are instantly ignited, producing a clean yellow flame and soon we are drinking cups of scalding water flavored with packets of Land O'Lakes hot chocolate mix I have bought at the ridiculous price of sixty-five cents apiece. Already I am counting the remaining packets and worrying. Will there be enough? Jeff carries the lunches and I the dinners. We've got plenty of freeze-dried backpacker food and lightweight Ramen-type noodles, but I have skimped a little on hot chocolate because I thought it weighed too much. But this is not a night to give sway to caution. We raise cup after reckless cup of chocolate and take turns saying, "Gentlemen, I give you the Gorge."

5

Little Colorado Day Two
Big Stone Potato Camp

It is very peaceful in the Canyon. The mornings are still, and in the blue-gray hours of dawn we understand keenly why we've come. But as we don our packs and begin our march, the crystal clarity of the answer flags. Day Two is an endless trudge over miles of cracked mud and around pockets of quicksand into which we sometimes carelessly slip, necessitating a tiring, frustrating extraction. Crawling on our bellies, dragging our heavy, mud-laden legs out of the muck is a misery which elicits the hike's hottest oaths. Standing in the sun, completely plastered with mud, I recall a science fiction movie I saw as a child in the fifties. In it, a hapless astronaut returns from space monstrously transformed by a heavy, clinging, silver substance encrusted on his space suit. He shuffles ponderously through the woods leaving luminous, glittery footprints and strangling anyone who gets in his way. For the first time I appreciate the pathos of his situation.

We reach the narrows early. Quicksand Alley. Here the cliffs rise high. Above us droop the remains of a thin, rickety suspension bridge with some blue sky showing through where spans are missing. The bridge was built by engineers who once considered damming the Gorge at this spot. This is a remnant of a time during which engineers plugged up every narrow place where water flowed, encouraged and admired by practically every man, woman and child in the country. It was a golden age or a time of excess, depending on your viewpoint, and there were few places these engineers didn't succeed in clogging up. Today, however, their support is waning. Granted, there was much gained by such projects, particularly in the control of flooding and the production of electrical power, but it was only later that the losses were thoughtfully tallied and weighed against the returns. In some cases, the numbers came up short.

Now there is a movement to restore some of the riparian environs lost during this time of license and, though no major dams have yet been dismantled, the effort continues. The most ambitious endeavor is the proposal to retire the great Glen Canyon Dam on the Colorado just seventy miles upstream from the mouth of the Gorge. It's a hard idea to sell. In 1964 the Bureau of Reclamation closed the flood gates of Glen Canyon Dam with the blessings and enthusiasm of a wide spectrum of society. There were only the few plaintive, impotent mutterings of an embryonic environmental movement that had yet to find its muscle. The Sierra Club's president Dave Brower had to choose between saving Glen Canyon or Dinosaur National Park which was simultaneously threatened with a dam. Brower did not know Glen Canyon. Hardly anyone did. By the time he found out what he was swapping, it was too late. Dinosaur was saved but not Glen Canyon. It was a sickening trade off, a mistake for which Brower would never forgive himself. From then on he adopted a harder attitude, one that would soon lead to the club's losing its tax-exempt status and becoming an organization with clout. It was that attitude which saved the Canyon. Two other dams were planned for within the Grand Canyon itself: Marble Canyon and Bridge Canyon dams whose construction would have caused appalling damage. When the compromise of building only one of them was suggested, the environmentalists held fast. No dams, period. The Grand Canyon was saved.

Glen Canyon Dam is a marvel of modern engineering, a testament to man's dominion over nature and a moneymaker to boot. Granted, as the waters rose and drowned forever the lovely tree-lined river and tributaries of the canyonlands, there might have escaped a sigh here and there from even the most enthusiastic of the dam's supporters. But whatever misgivings might have stirred in the shallow waters of their conscience, there was solace in the thought that all was inevitable. After all, progress had to be allowed.

Not many years later, as the import of the disaster became clear, it dawned on even some supporters of the dam that what had been done might not have been such a good idea. Did the short term electrical gain justify the destruction of a wilderness of timeless unsurpassed beauty? Moreover, the thousands of drowned archeological sites might have also been undervalued. The hopes that the lake would bring great recreational opportunities fell flat. The greatest attractions were underwater! A million acres of them were replaced by a featureless plane of fetid water quickly filling with silt and in places sometimes too contaminated to swim in. The fraction of land above, sad little islands, remained accessible only by expensive power boats. Indeed, the water so drastically narrowed the possibilities that recreation was limited almost exclusively to the boaty set. Hiking, hunting, bird watching, rafting, climbing, exploring, all were gone. Even a unique fishing possibility was lost. The great Colorado River squawfish, so ready to take a bait, and sometimes reaching a length of five feet, was reduced to a number hardly worth the counting. The wondrous slot canyons, all but the Paria, were flooded. Every bird, every mountain lion, every bobcat, every ringtail, every lizard and kingsnake, was either drowned or run out forever. The great cottonwoods stood in icy darkness, their leaves long since turned to mud. This realization might have been a shock, much as a hanging might later make restive those who had, with great alacrity, lynched an innocent man. But the subtle inferences of the error of Glen Canyon Dam remained lost on most, and still do, passing at best like a troubling but evanescent breeze.

How is the notion of draining the reservoir being received? When the Sierra Club first announced its position, the reaction in newspapers was surprising. As one would expect, many ridiculed the idea as completely crazy. More than a few columnists, however, reacted thoughtfully, conceding that what now seems outrageously audacious may one day make sense much in the same way the notion of an integrated army, or automobile seat belts, now seem reasonable. Even the late Barry Goldwater admitted his 20/20 hindsight and confessed his regret for having supported the dam. "Water is important," he said. "But not that important."

The proponents do not underestimate the boldness of the idea. But while the legal ramifications of the thing are daunting, the mechanics are ostensibly simple. The proposal is to open the gates and slowly drain the reservoir over the span of a decade or more. Then would come the challenging restoration project. At first there would be revealed a landscape rivaling the wasteland wrought by the eruption of Mount St. Helens. It would be a depressing sight, but it needn't remain so. Much of the restoration would be accomplished by the reviving Glen Canyon itself. In his essay "The Damnation of a Canyon," Edward Abbey offered encouraging words: "...give nature a little time. In five years, at most in ten, the sun and wind and storms will cleanse and sterilize the repellent mess... Within a generation—thirty years I predict—the river and canyons will bear a decent resemblance to their former selves. Within the lifetime of our children, Glen Canyon, the living river, the heart of the Canyonlands, will be restored to us."

There are some who are convinced that all the debate may be unnecessary. They contend that the leaky sandstone either side of Glen Canyon Dam may ultimately fail and drain the reservoir on its own. If the events of 1983 are any indication, they might be right. In June of that year the dam's operators foolishly allowed unusually heavy runoff to get ahead of them. Before they knew it, the unthinkable was happening. More water was spilling into the lake than they could release. At first they tried running the turbines continuously at maximum output, but this was not nearly enough. They then began routing the water around the turbines by opening four outlet tubes, but this still could not keep pace with the filling reservoir. There was soon no option but to open the two gargantuan spillway tunnels. These had been carved into the living rock and lined with steel reinforced concrete, and through them 200,000 cubic feet per second could be released. This should have provided a way out of the jam, but a complication arose. The thundering hydraulics through the spillways were tearing away the concrete lining of the tunnels along with huge chunks of Navajo Sandstone. A process called cavitation was digging immense troughs into the stone itself. The spillways were literally falling apart. The engineers dared not continue a full release but neither could they allow the dam to be breached. They cut the flow through the spillways, letting loose as much water as they dared. By the 28th of June the operators of the dam were releasing 92,200 cfs while Lake Powell was filling at 116,000 cfs. You didn't need a Ph.D. in mathematics to figure it out; the lake was going to spill over the dam. As a desperate, last ditch effort, engineers put into place a plan born of panic and necessity. Large sheets of top-of-the-line plywood were erected to plug the river above the spillway gates, raising the level of Lake Powell by an astonishing four feet. This bought enough time to ride out the crisis and avert a disaster which might well have included the loss of the entire dam. While the Bureau of Reclamation insists that the dam was not at any time in danger of failing, few downstream could have felt much security knowing that the titanic Lake Powell was held in check by a jury-rigged assembly of plywood sheets.

All told, if the supporters of the dam are doing any worrying, it's premature. The idea of draining the reservoir is pretty close to an impossible dream at present and the implications are far-ranging and complex. Now that what's done is done, it is hard for even devoted environmentalists to agree on whether it should be attempted or not. Draining Lake Powell may be an idea whose time will come, but it is a long way down the road. Still, panicky supporters of the reservoir erected billboard signs in and around Phoenix. They shrieked:

DON'T LET THE SIERRA CLUB DRAIN LAKE POWELL!

Naturally, it was a moment's work for monkey-wrenchers, who don't much groove on billboard signs in the first place, to black out with paint all but the last three words.

Ten miles in we hear voices. They are coming from the first overlook off Highway 64 where it threads up to Grand Canyon National Park and Desert View Watch Tower. We can see little dabs of color—people leaning on railings that seem a thousand feet above us. A steep path called the Sheep Trail enters somewhere near this lookout, one of the few places where one may enter the Gorge. We had peered over these same railings yesterday where the Gorge is deep and narrow and foreboding; it was with a certain trepidation that I had pictured myself walking across the sands far below. Now I imagine that the tiny specks of green and blue Kelty nylon, moving along, add an element of the picturesque to the scene for those above if indeed anyone notices us.

There are deer tracks here and for a while I attempt to let them show me the path of least resistance. But it doesn't work. A mule deer is up higher and doesn't skirt places the same way as a hiker. A mule deer doesn't feel compelled to weave in and out between rocks and brush and is not in the least bit afraid of getting his feet wet. We come across several mule deer as we walk and once, detouring over a sandy, tree-covered delta, we discover a small dead one whose sad ears jut out of a pile of dusty, fur-covered bones like little felt slippers.

We carry in the convenient side pockets of our Kelty packs 50-ounce plastic suck-top bottles filled with yellow or brown mudhole water, thoughtfully poisoned with double doses of iodine. No need to carry more. There is plenty of water—little crescents along the banks or deep pockets in the shade of boulders. I had worried that the water would be warm and fetid, but it is quite cool, tastes fine. I have been warned that the water here might be radioactive, contaminated by the tailings of uranium mines and toxic spills upstream. But there is nothing that can be done about it. In one puddle I find a handful of dead minnows. Muddy as it makes things, the abundance of water is a blessing in that it allows us to walk burdened only by the weight of one small bottle each.

We cross mile after mile of mud cracks and boulders and river stones, resting often in the shade of cottonwoods, and as we descend, the Gorge narrows and the timeless songs of canyon wrens echo from the cliffs. The water-rounded cobblestones in the Gorge make for safe walking as the plastic foundation they rest upon has allowed them to settle together nicely. Cemented securely in the hard silt, they seldom wobble.

Jeff is keeping track of birds. Among those recorded on his list are blue grosbeaks, lesser goldfinches, yellow warblers, yellow-rumped warblers, violet-green swallows, black-tailed gnatcatchers, a snowy egret, assorted turkey buzzards, ravens, and miraculous white-throated swifts.

The swifts are a wonder. Perhaps you'll remember, if you're of the right vintage, those little plastic delta-winged airplanes that came with a stick and a long rubber band when you were a kid. They don't make them anymore, of course, because they were the perfect recipe for putting out a child's eye forever. But if you recall the way those little planes sliced the air in long graceful sweeps, you'll have an idea of how the white-throated swift flies. These birds rarely land; they even mate on the wing. When they are thirsty, they jet down low and skim water from pools. On hilltops in the desert, they sometimes shoot past so fast you'd think an arrow just missed your head.

We crunch along toward Hellhole Bend, a couple of torsions in the Gorge, but it's hard to make out any landmarks. To us, every turn looks like a Hellhole Bend and we are damned if we can tell the difference. In places we can see how truly steep the grade of the tributary is, for we are looking almost downhill to jumbles of boulders. From time to time we must negotiate boulder fields, winding our way through, always looking to see if our path is leading us to a dry, crossable spot where quicksand won't force us to back-track. After a while I develop a sense of the land and as I walk it seems I never make a mistake, always choosing the route requiring the least effort and the one that leads to dry ground. At last we reach what we are fairly certain is Hellhole Bend. It is steeper and more twisted than what has come before.

It was here that Harvey Butchart in a 1964 foot survey of the Gorge recounted a dramatic discovery—a twenty foot shock wave crater radiating from a hole five feet deep where a block of stone the size of a grand piano had fallen 950 feet and smacked into wet sand. Outside the boundaries of geologic time, rock falls are rare. We have seen the evidence of them in the canyon often. Downcanyon they will be most apparent in the Redwall Limestone, a pale strata stained red by the layers above. The sections where rock has cracked loose from the cliffs and fallen away are obvious, for the bright unstained interior of the rock is exposed.

Farther down, we stop and lean our packs against a block of stone as big as a house. It's late but we have made up for the short day before, having traveled a good 17 miles. Now we're hungry as hell. We sit in the cool shade with our backs against the tremendous block, too tired for the moment to cook. A tiger swallowtail butterfly flutters silently by.

Not far downstream, the Indian Maiden Route begins at the east side of the Gorge and exits on the opposite side of the river where it climbs out as the Moody Route. If the Blue Spring, Horse and Salt trails are more routes than trails, Indian Maiden and Moody are entirely routes; there is no trail to them at all; they are just "ways" to get from one side of the Gorge to the other. Five hundred feet below the rim on Indian Maiden Route, hiker Bill Orman discovered a name etched on the rock in old style script: *E Holmes*; nearby was an older marking, a petroglyph in the shape of a Mudhead Kachina.

The gradient at Hellhole Bend is pronounced. During flooding this stretch of the canyon becomes a cauldron of thrashing mud, runnable only by the most audacious of kayakers. The Gorge was first paddled by Brad Dimock and Tim Cooper in 1978 during a rainy spell of weather which had turned the tributary into a rumbling river. The twenty-five-year-olds faced some particular problems as they entered the stream at the Cameron Bridge. To begin with, there was the possibility of drowning in the current. The Gorge had never been run in its entirety before and no one knew whether it was navigable or not. The Gorge is much narrower than the Grand Canyon, and its gradient three times as steep as the Colorado River's. During flooding the Gorge carries a volume rivaling that of the main course. Cooper and Dimock had also heard disconcerting rumors of unavoidable fifty-foot falls. But an excess of water was not their only concern. The inverse of the situation was another possible factor—the river might simply dry up underneath their kayaks, stranding them in the middle of a fifty-seven mile highway of impassable, knee-deep mud. This had happened to a previous pair of kayakers who attempted the run. It took them nine days to reach the confluence on foot.

There was another troubling aspect of the trip that warranted consideration—the law. The odds of acquiring a legal permit to run the Colorado River through the Grand Canyon are roughly the same as being hit by a flying saucer. Upon reaching the confluence, Dimock and Cooper would be in violation and any ranger worth his salt, they knew, could make a graceful metamorphosis from naturalist to cop in an instant. Big fine. Threat of jail. From Tim Cooper's account of the trip though, it appears that the young men's strategy was to figure out that problem when they got there. Arriving at the Colorado alive was the first order of business.

The initial few miles were easy paddling. They floated through the narrows and deeper into the Gorge. Beginning at mile seven, however, the course to the confluence was a dangerous, exhausting traverse of furious brown water plunging over boulders. They continued on and on through the Gorge. Below Blue Spring they navigated some perilous travertine cascades, even one dramatically christened Atomizer Falls, but there were no fifty-foot plunges. The Little Colorado River Gorge was runnable, but just barely. Three days later, the two kayakers reached the Colorado at mile 61 and glided onto the big river. But word was out on them. Cold, wet, tired and hungry, they were happy enough to be busted near Hance Rapid.

From my food bag I remove two cardboard-bottomed packets of freeze-dried green peas. Unfolded, these become freestanding containers of flimsy, but cook-safe, clear plastic into which we stir boiling water. We let the peas rehydrate for a minute or two and then add a pouch of four-cheese Idahoan instant mashed potato mix to each. The mixture is thin at first, but the powder suddenly solidifies around the spoon and becomes a rich, pasty conglomerate of peas and potatoes. It is here, in our great hunger, that we first experience the Blueberry Newton Effect. Anyone who has backpacked any distance will recognize it.

The term was coined during a trip Jeff took a year ago in the Pecos Wilderness in New Mexico. He was at the end of an exhausting ten-day trek when a companion produced a package of Blueberry Newtons and handed them out to the famished troops. The chewing of these mushy cookies evoked such a feeling of comfort and beauty that the hikers, all of them, lay back on the dusty trail and closed their eyes in grateful ecstasy. Their lower jaws made slow sensuous circles as the little cakes dissolved, and they smacked their lips and tasted their tongues and uttered little whimpers of astonished delight. All were possessed by the conviction that they were in the presence of a benevolent, living God.

Such feelings of longing and gratitude were evoked by

these Newtons that their thoughts became loving and sentimental and they thought of philanthropy and the meaning of
truth. Then they reproached themselves harshly that they
should have lived so long and been such fools as to have never known about Blueberry Newtons and some of them stood
and confessed on the spot, and swore that upon their return
their cupboards would be packed as taut as snare drums with
boxes of Blueberry Newtons so that they should never be
without them. Their empty, shallow lives would henceforth
be free of such grievous omissions from then on and forever,
so help them God. Some have boxes of Blueberry Newtons
petrifying on their shelves today.

And so it is with our green peas and cheese potatoes.
The Gorge is silent. We rest in the cool half dark of evening
against the gigantic stone and eat our heavenly mashed potato feast.

6
Little Colorado Day Three
Glugging Springs

Our 17-mile march yesterday has given us confidence and we are determined to reach Blue Spring today. We are on a tight schedule. Jeff has to return to Texas on Sunday morning so we must complete the trek in only eight days. Were we photographers this would be difficult, as it would be impossible not to stop and linger for hours waiting for the perfect light. The Gorge is packed with surfaces and textures that photographers like: the multifarious designs of mud cracks, crescent silt, and sandstone compositions where the rock is like pale sanded pine with all the swirls and rivers of wood grain flowing. Green bushes grow from little hills of red alluvium or damp gray mud, and the banks are colored by purple flowering arrow weed and the pink, feathery floreates of tamarisks growing out of staircases of hardened sand. Jeff and I carry four 27-shot disposable cameras rattling around in our packs and we stop marching from time to time to click our plastic shutters. The cliffs of the Gorge soar a thousand feet above us and more—massive, as solid as iron, stained black with desert varnish.

There is no sign that hikers have been here. No campfire rings, no footprints, no Power Bar wrappers. The Gorge is ours. There is, however, the flotsam from upstream: a tire, an empty insulin bottle, and more often than I would have liked, black or yellow motor oil bottles whisked here by floods. We also come upon children's toys washed in from above: the treaded wheel of a toy truck wedged between two rocks, a doll crucified surreally in a tamarisk, and a little rubber fish which swam the Gorge and didn't quite make the confluence before the river dried up.

We note the wildlife: black-tailed gnatcatchers, a blue-winged teal, and tarantula hawks—huge orange-winged wasps, whose dark metallic blue legs hang heavily. Startled mule deer clamber through the mesquite and bound over the brush and boulders like kangaroos. As we walk by, angry battalions of spiders storm out of deep mud cracks and sometimes, from the same cracks, struggle clumsy little toads. In a crevasse in the silt we find the dry, sombrous mummy of a bat and in the pools, always, cheerful swarms of black pollywogs swimming in the water stirring up tiny whirlwinds of tan mud in the bright sunlight.

Today we must navigate through fields of boulders and make detours around quicksand bordering the yellow pools and brown mudholes. Jeff's feet are a mess, but he doesn't complain. During each break, he has been dabbing his feet with Neosporin and taping swaths of plastic cut from Ziploc bags over the worst areas. He has discarded the boots and is now wearing running shoes, an old beat-up pair he brought for around-camp use, but they are full of holes. Sand and gravel and mud have gotten in and made things worse. I have great confidence in my shoes, an old resoled pair of Italian Zamberlans.

Just past Waterhole Canyon at mile 35, we hear the gurgle of running water. At first we don't understand what it means, and then we find in a narrow passage within the Redwall Limestone, clear springs glugging into the wash. The aquifer in the Gorge, we know, is saturated with dissolved carbonates, but when we taste the spring water where it spills in little falls over the sand, we find it only vaguely salty. It will be good from now on to drink clear water. Still, we treat it with iodine. Some hikers carry special filters designed to strain out the microscopic wildlife and others, in order to avoid the iodine taste, carry little dropper bottles of regular household bleach. A few drops per quart, they claim, purifies water as well as iodine and leaves no aftertaste.

We make camp immediately on the sand near the springs, and though we haven't reached our goal of Blue Spring, we are content knowing that it is only five miles away. We are very satisfied with the camp. Just above the Redwall on the left, a stone Madonna holding a child peers down and there are smooth flats of silt to sleep on. The evening falls; the Gorge turns gray. We cook freeze-dried lasagna and turkey tetrazini and top off the night with hot chocolate which, charmed by the powerful alchemy of the Blueberry Newton Effect, has become an indescribably bewitching ambrosia.

7

Little Colorado Day Four
Blue Spring North

It's Tuesday and we get a late start. A half hour of walking and I feel a curious sensation, a tiny irritation on my heel. Must be a hot spot, I think. Time to patch it with moleskin. Don't want to end up like Jeff. I sit on a stone and remove my boot and sock. "Good God. It's already a blister!" Big as a nickel. I cover it with moleskin and within a hundred feet it has broken open. Forty-five miles to go. From here on that blister is going to harass me, torment me, get worse. But there's nothing to do about it. I secretly curse my Zamberlans for letting me down. Truth be told, it is probably not the fault of the shoes. Sand and mud and bits of gravel accumulating in my socks are probably the cause. My brother keeps quiet. He suspects that all along I've been keeping my big flapper shut about his getting a blister at mile three of an eighty-mile hike. I had warned him ahead of time to bring good shoes and he opted to wear the same ones that gave him grief on our trip down the Tanner years ago. "It kind of snuck up on me," I explained.

Jeff carries one of those ultra lightweight sleeping pads—the kind that makes for wonderfully comfortable sleeping if there isn't a pebble under you bigger than a BB. But he has discovered a use for it. The substance is easily cut with scissors to create little pads, rather like mole foam. I stuff a wide, horseshoe-shaped chunk in the back of my boot and it relieves the pressure on the blister, sort of.

We reach Blue Spring at one o'clock and take sensational plunges into the cold, azure water. Divided by twenty feet of fallen stone slabs, Blue Spring gushes out in two main sections. The clear water swirls into the Gorge creating not just a stream but a real river, three times bigger than Grand Canyon's famous Havasu Creek. While it is not shrouded with maidenhair fern as I had imagined, it is still an enchanting spring with deep, blue pools and pale, sandy shallows. We lounge and float and dream for two hours at this rarely visited jewel.

While the water of Blue Spring is pretty, it has a bad reputation. It has been reported by hiker John Annerino as "...practically unpalatable unless doctored with EGR or some other powdered drink mix–unless you're in a dire emergency." Hiking legend Harvey Butchart in a 1965 article in *Arizona Highways* also spoke poorly of it:

> "...the flavor of the water is a disagreeable mixture of table salt and Epsom salt. The tincture is weak and a doctor has declared it safe to drink indefinitely. I have used it for thirty-six hours, but the flavor becomes increasingly repugnant, and I was glad to dip my canteen again in the muddy Colorado."

So maligned has been the spring's reputation that in

1956 two park rangers, Kit Wing and Les Womack, hauled five gallons of drinking water down Blue Spring Trail to their camp at the floor of the Gorge. Their object was to raft a segment of the Little C to the confluence and this necessitated their lugging a sixty pound inflatable boat down the trail as well. Their ingress, Blue Spring Trail, is a steep, potentially dangerous route requiring at times the use of a rope to descend. The rangers were successful in their rafting traverse and were able to reach the confluence and, after several portages of rapids in the Colorado, the foot of the Tanner Trail where they hauled out all their gear including the boat. I can't help thinking, however, that their lugging water from the rim was a wasted effort.

Contrary to finding the water barely drinkable, we enjoy clear, fresh spring water perceiving only the slightest Alka-Seltzer taste. In fact, the water gushing from the rock is so cold and lovely that I dispense with the iodine routine entirely. It seems inconceivable that water issuing from a rupture in the rock purified by thousands of feet of stone in such a remote area could not be safe to drink.

We are reluctant to leave Blue Spring, but, with our schedule, a five-mile total for one day is not enough. There is no passage along the shore for much of the remaining fifteen miles of river and the parts that are passable make for the most laborious and grueling walking. From here on, we will be wading across or swimming the river often. But I've thought this out ahead of time. Before our trip, I purchased two inflatable neoprene swimming doughnuts, the kind of colorful toys children use at the beach or in the pool. We remove them from our packs, blow them up, and tie a length of twine to each. Then we lay them on the water and carefully position our packs on top. It is great fun walking along through the sand-bottomed shallows with our packs (which are most welcomely not on our backs) moving effortlessly alongside us in the current, encouraged only occasionally by a lazy tug on the strings. In the deep sections we swim next to our buoyant companions with our toes skimming the sandy bottom. Easy on the back, these stretches, and easier on the feet. We grin like yokels. We imagine floating like this all the way to the confluence and, with the wishful wings of optimism, bid farewell to aching backs and footsore trudging, to hot, dry skin rasped by shoulder straps, and imagine a new life of cool drifting. But soon the current becomes swifter, boulder fields appear and we are faced with travertine dams and other hazards to navigation. My pack rebounds gently off a boulder in the stream and makes a short, wobbling, but safe slide into a pool. Jeff follows and also accomplishes a safe passage. And so we continue, experiencing only a few mishaps. Along a slow, gentle stretch, I drop the string attached to my little raft and trust the river. I stride weightlessly across the smooth, silty shore a long way ahead as the current carries my pack over dark blue water ten feet deep. I find a shady spot and sit on the sand until the pack comes to me like a faithful hound.

Blue Spring North is a shady camp on a sand bar with a grove of tamarisks and mesquites handy for hanging up items to dry in the hot wind. As the sky darkens, the wind abates and the canyon cools. My notebook for this evening has a single notation: "One orangish falling star."

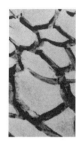

8

Horse Trail Blues
May 27, 2002

In April of 1994 a woman fell fifty feet off the Blue Spring Trail. Cheryl Soshnik of Park City, Utah had logged a lot of time on the Grand Canyon's more remote trails but this was her first look at the Blue Spring Route. She was at the beginning of an eight-day Gorge hike and carried on her back a 65-pound external frame Kelty pack. This was lucky. The pack, stuffed full of gear and the snapping aluminum frame, absorbed the shock of the impact, cutting her losses to multiple compound fractures of the arms, a lacerated liver and a pneumothorax. That the heavy pack and all its cushioning properties spared her life sings rather small in light of the fact that without it she probably wouldn't have fallen at all. The spot from which she fell was not especially scary. Certainly not anything like the big drop-off she had edged around near the top. It was not a place one would expect to fall off. Still, a loose patch of gravel and some extra water sloshing in a container at the top of her pack conspired to throw her off balance. Help was not quick in coming. Part of two days and a whole night were spent waiting. As a paramedic herself, Soshnik knew that the percentages were not particularly in her favor. She worried that she might "bleed out" during the night, but her luck held. Her senses, perhaps heightened by a desire to survive, had become so acute that late the next morning she detected, minutes before anyone else, the distant chopping blades of the rescue helicopter. Seven surgeries later, she would return to finish the hike, but not before a stopover in Orabi to visit a Hopi Medicine Woman to dulcify the spirits of the Gorge. Soshnik wasn't particularly superstitious but, after what happened to her, she figured it couldn't hurt.

All this in mind, I am just a little wary of exploring the Blue Spring Trail. After all, if an experienced canyoneer could fall, so could I. My plan is to locate the Horse trailhead, hike down to the spring and then explore up the Blue Spring Trail. But I won't be packing any sixty-five pounds. This won't take much doing. Try as I might, I can't get a pack to weigh much more than thirty-five pounds even with a full supply of water and a week's worth of food. To reach a sixty-five pound total I'd have to add items every bit equal to the weight of a case and a half of beer. Naturally, I take all prudent steps to lighten the load. I leave the cast iron skillet at home, along with that big flashlight I own, the one like those bouncers use at night clubs to check IDs—the kind full of D batteries which doubles as a billy club—and the four-burner Coleman stove. Also, like anyone, I trim the weight by packing freeze-dried food and lightweight noodles. Aside from that, the only extra trimming I do is to carry a featherweight wood-burning Zip Stove or "Sierra" which eliminates the need to carry fuel.

The Camp Dragon, which I have already mentioned in passing, is my own version of the Zip. While I'm not much interested in hiking equipment, the Zip Stove captured my imagination. It'll burn anything you find lying around and do it so efficiently that just a small bundle of twigs, a little pile of bark or a few pinecones can cook dinner in a jiffy. For a long, unsupported hike, what could be smarter than a stove with an unlimited fuel supply—a supply you don't have to carry? The parsimonious Zip also allows for an ecologically friendly campfire, one that blackens no rocks, leaves no ugly charcoal mess and hardly taxes the environment's supply of wood. It had become one of my regrets that I was not its inventor. I did, as I mentioned, design a different version.

The Camp Dragon, as my small son named it, came about as the result of an injury I sustained a year before our through hike of the Gorge, an injury which somehow triggered a manic state and launched me into a frenzied project of design science. The injury was the result of a poorly executed swan dive off the high dive at the local public pool and it required surgery. I remember lying on a gurney ready to go under the knife.

"Which shoulder is it again?" asked the nurse.

"The right."

This was the third time I'd been asked.

"You guys are afraid you'll cut the wrong shoulder, aren't you?"

"Not really," she lied.

With a black magic marker she scrawled in bold letters NO on my left shoulder and YES on the right and I awoke some hours later with three scope holes, a drain tube hanging out of my back and a large sewn-up wound along the top of the correct shoulder.

"How're you feeling?"

"It's my rotor cap, Doc," I said, the lingering anesthesia blurring somewhat the distinction between anatomical and automotive. Actually, it was a torn rotator cuff. The surgery was a routine procedure. The operation involved opening up the shoulder, drilling holes into the humerus, hammering in little steel tent stakes and sewing everything back where it belonged.

It was during my convalescence that I tackled with great manic alacrity my project to create my own rendition of the classic Zip. My goal was to make a similar contraption which was smaller, lighter and more efficient. I wasn't much of a handyman. I slashed myself with sheet metal, banged my thumb with a ball peen hammer and found I had a great talent for being unable to locate tools I had only just put down a second ago. These were not small tools like tiny Allen wrenches or screwdrivers, but big metal shears, hammers and power tools which would vanish and then reappear like fairies under my chair or in a blind spot near my elbow or in places I couldn't even remember having been. The floor of the garage remained covered for weeks by a landslide of sheet metal shards, discarded tools, spilled nuts, bolts, washers and brackets, wire, and stalagmites of dripped solder.

I experimented with many kinds of miniature fans and motors for the blower unit. Tiny computer cooling fans with their neat assemblies seemed to have great promise but they proved inefficient. They were power-hungry little devils that drew nine to twelve volts out of expensive batteries which cried uncle after two minutes at best. The answer was the tried and true little three-volt motor which the Zip Stove utilized, a tiny powerhouse with a ninety-nine-cent price tag at Radio Shack. It had a reputation for never breaking down and ran practically forever on one AA battery.

With tin snips I made an excellent little fan out of the top off a small can of Contadina tomato paste which I attached securely to the motor with a little sleeve collar. Then I shortened the can itself, and using brackets and tiny nuts, assembled the motor and fan securely within. Finally, I attached a stout three-position click switch, a resistor for low speed (simmering) and a plastic snap-in battery holder and there was my blower.

Designing the rest of the gadget was trickier. There were all kinds of unforeseeable problems. For example, the apparatus had a tendency to create a back draft and suck in flames which threatened to burn up the fan and motor. It was a while before I hit on a simple way to construct the burner's vent so that a tongue of fire could not stab back into the blower. The burner itself was a small, heavy gauge roast beef stew can with a two-inch circular hole baffled by a circle of sheet metal pierced by eight air holes.

The supports for the cooking pot were four inverted mirror hangers secured by wing nuts. Because the supports had two holes, they could be adjusted to two different heights and they folded back into the burner. The separate blower stowed away in the burner as well and the whole cylinder was neatly topped with the plastic cover off a coffee can. Along with the Camp Dragon name, my son supplied a Pokemon sticker of a dragon blowing flames to decorate the plastic cap. The end result was a four-by-four-inch stove with a two-by-three-inch blower unit which weighed in at eight ounces. Unlike the Zip, my two-piece Camp Dragon did not operate with the burner wobbling atop the blower, but rather received the charge of air from the side via the separate snap-on fan unit.

I sat for hours admiring the symmetry of its design, its rugged construction, and marveling that I should ever have been able to create something so wonderful. Then the pyrophoric fever of the experience waned along with what I worry were bipolar symptoms, and the Camp Dragon became just another ridiculous piece of backpacker junk and I stowed it in my pack where it would be ready when I needed it.

As it turned out, the Horse Trail is not after all so hard to find if you have good directions. The first time I looked for it a few years ago, I took a wrong turn off a wide tribal road and got lost. A Navajo rancher followed me down a faint track to find out what I was doing out there.

"Trespassing!" his wife said from the pickup.

The husband and I stood alongside the little road.

I fumbled with my maps. "I'm looking for the Horse Trail," I said. "Is this Waterhole Canyon?"

"I only know the Navajo name. You shouldn't be out here without a permit."

Naturally, I was a little defensive.

"I'm just trying to find a place, not up to any mischief or anything."

"Yeah, well, I don't know that," he explained.

"Sorry. Is it all right if I look around a little?"

"There's nothing here, guy."

He was very civil but his voice held an unmistakable tone of finality. I apologized and left. A permit might well have mollified him. I was figuring I'd find the trailhead first and then get a permit. But he had me. I had once lived on the Navajo Reservation for two years and understood a little. Navajos are about the nicest people you'll meet, but it's still their land.

In May of 2002 I was back. With me was Tom Jilek, a neighbor who had never backpacked before. This time I had a permit and excellent step-by-step directions sent to me by Bill Orman of Tuba City, a member of the Grand Canyon Hikers Email group, with whom I had been corresponding. Like many of the members on this group, Orman was not only devoted to the Grand Canyon, its history and its preservation, but to its tributaries as well. He was one of a handful of people who had hiked all three routes into the Gorge. He was extremely knowledgeable and enthusiastically shared what he knew. When I told him I was taking a first time backpacker he e-mailed: "I would be hesitant taking the neighbor. You would do fine on this trip solo. I have had mixed, even frightening experiences in the Canyon with untested hikers."

But I really wasn't worried. Tom was an ex-marine,

almost ten years younger than me, and in excellent shape. My main worry was that he wouldn't enjoy the hike. It would be hotter than blazes and I knew the trail was a rough one. Beyond that, this kind of hiking requires a certain mindset, a kind of stoicism where the rewards of the experience are measured against a certain amount of misery. Most people wouldn't like it.

We arrive at the trailhead just after noon, park the big rented Impala and start down with the sun cooking our faces. The Horse Trail descends through a canyon just downstream of Waterhole Canyon. At the floor of the Gorge I know we will find brooklets of water running down from Glugging Springs, but since the desert hiking adage dictates, "hike *from* water, not *to* water," I have stashed two gallons in the trunk of the car. I only hope the brand new Chevy is still there and in one piece when we get back. The trailhead is in the middle of nowhere and there have been instances when the local version of juvenile delinquents have vandalized vehicles left at such secluded locations.

We scramble down into the shallow upper part of the canyon past clusters of beehive cactus, pass through a small pour-off, and walk the wash down to a dizzying precipice above the Coconino Sandstone. The trail winds around to the right under a long, curving overhang and zigzags down a scree slope to a wash where we boulder-hop following sparsely placed cairns. A chunk of pottery alongside the path confirms that this route is an old one, but the trail itself is more recent. Exactly who built it is hard to know, but it is thought

Trailhead for the Horse Trail. Photos: S.Cole.

Steve on the Salt Trail.

After entering the Gorge near Cameron Bridge.

Jeff in the Gorge.

Jeff floating his pack.

Jeff pausing.

The Madonna above Glugging Springs.

Travertine mound.

*Above: Camp in the LCR
Gorge north of Blue Spring.*

Left: Steve beside the LCR.

Blue Spring.

Just downstream of Blue Spring.

Crossing the LCR.

Beamer Cabin remains beside the Little Colorado.
Photo: T. Martin.

Confluence with the Colorado River from Chuar Butte.
Photo: T. Martin.

that it was once used to bring stock to water in the Gorge.

Quartz crystals grow in small rings on some of the rocks looking a little like fossil crinoids. I also find some round concretions and a little geode which I smack open with a stone exposing a shallow pocket decorated by a sparkling array of miniature crystals. Bill Orman has told me to look for bighorn sheep in this branch of the Gorge but we see none.

Tom, who is hiking in tennis shoes, must tread carefully for there are hedgehog cactus here and there. I also see a great many datura plants with large white trumpet-shaped flowers, *Datura stratemonia*. The species was one of artist Georgia O'keefe's favorites and its blossoms the subject of many of her paintings. Datura is notable not just for its beauty. If you tear a datura leaf, it exudes a smell like peanut butter, and if eaten, smoked, or brewed as tea and drunk, tropane belladonna alkaloids in the sap will produce colorful hallucinations. Unfortunately, the pretty pictures are, often enough, followed by delirium and death from anticholinergic poisoning. The plant has been utilized for thousands of years as a religious conduit into the spirit world, as an aphrodisiac, as a medicine and, of course, as a poison. The plant is also called sacred datura, moonflower, thorn apple, devil's weed or jimson weed. Jimson is a corruption of the word Jamestown where in 1676 during Bacon's Rebellion, British troops were accidentally poisoned after eating a dinner containing the plant. Robert Beverly in his 1705 *History of Virginia* described the antics of the intoxicated men, a performance predating the Three Stooges by two hundred and sixty years:

"...they turned natural fools upon it for several days: one would blow a feather in the air; another would dart straws at it with much fury, and another, stark naked, would fondly kiss and paw his companions. In this frantic condition they were confined, lest they should in their folly, destroy themselves. "

While the men eventually came to their senses and suffered no lasting ill effects, datura is a bad choice for recreational use. No part of the plant is not poisonous and even if one survives the trip, the neurological damage can be profound and permanent. At least one death in the Grand Canyon is attributed to the plant. In 1971 a hiker at Phantom Ranch ingested the drug in the form of tea brewed from datura flowers. His symptoms were similar to the Jamestown diners but unlike them, he was not adequately confined. He wound up in the river. His body was found five weeks later miles downstream.

Less insidious botanicals also grow among the rocks along the Horse Trail: blossoming orange globemallow, Mormon tea and little white daisy-like flowers called fleabane. Small lizards skitter over rocks. In addition, we see two large collared lizards and a grand chuckwalla with a rusty pink tail as fat as a carrot. The collared lizards here have a dusty, yellowish tinge and an ocher tail, unlike collared lizards I've observed before which are sometimes as green as frogs.

The canyon soars up behind us and we turn to see the huge drop-off towering in the distance. Following cairns, we reach a group of split blocks, a rock window and an elaborate little bridge constructed of stout poles and flat slabs of stone along a ledge. Beyond, we find a stepladder made of sticks and stones that assists you around a point. The wood of these configurations is gray with age but, as we cross, both bridge and stepladder prove solid. How old the structures are is difficult to judge. Thirty-eight years ago Harvey Butchart traveled through this canyon beginning an upstream hike to Cameron. He mentioned nothing of them in his detailed 1965 article in *Arizona Highways*.

The sun is high and I'm burning up. We take a long lunch break in the shade above another drop-off near the bottom of the canyon. From here it's an easy scramble down. The canyon floor is much drier than last year. The footing is good. All the same, we camp early along the stream three miles above Blue Spring and rest our aching downhill muscles. I haven't carried a big pack in a year. The water flowing here from Glugging Springs is slow. As you'll recall, these nondescript little springs lie at mile 35, and issue from the Redwall on the right bank. Black and Say's phoebes rule this part of the Gorge. I watch as they catch insects, making their forays from rocks in the stream.

In the morning we walk down to Blue Spring. On the way we notice footprints in the mud of the river bed. One set (judging from the size, a woman's) are barefoot. Hiker Mike Mahany reported that in October he followed a set of barefoot prints from mile eleven all the way to Blue Spring—thirty-one miles! Soon we come to a recent rock fall. Red blocks the size of televisions are embedded in the wet sand and all around lie the jagged shards of stones that have shattered on river boulders. We ford the stream several times, stepping on rocks until there is no other option but to wade. In the shadows, dark water edged with green and yellow algae pours out of springs on the right bank and from the cliff faces bulge immense, drooping formations of travertine, some dry and extinct and others stained with beards of black algae, still sweating the calcareous water that formed them.

We follow thin paths through the dry, brushy deltas bordering the stream. Here in the hot, puffy silt lie the whirlpool sand traps of ant lions, some as big around as snuff cans. Tom has never seen them before. I am always surprised that so many people are unaware of these interesting little insects and their simple traps. Commonly called doodlebugs, ant lions are the larval form of a flying insect of the family *Myrmeleontidae* (from the Greek myrmex, meaning ant, and leon meaning lion). They spend much of their lives in the wingless stage under the sand catching small ants which slip into their conical pits. Eventually ant lions pupate and their imago fly away to reproduce.

References to the insect are found in abundance throughout history and literature. Mark Twain, to cite an instance, recorded a little doodlebug folk magic in his novel *The Adventures of Tom Sawyer*. In order to confirm his suspicions that witches were abroad, Twain's young protagonist speaks into the little whirlpool of sand:

> "...Doodlebug, doodlebug, tell me what I want to know!" The sand began to work and presently a

small black (sic) bug appeared for a second and then darted under again in a fright. "He dasn't tell! So it was a witch that done it. I just knowed it."

As a boy I had also been fascinated by ant lions. One summer I captured, with the help of a spoon and a wire kitchen strainer, a half dozen specimens and kept them as pets in a yellow King Edward cigar box full of sand. My experience with ant farms had been disappointing, but these insects were a smashing success. So impressive were their feedings that even my parents would invite guests into my room so they could see the creatures eat. I was always more than happy to show them off. I would quickly collect some black pismires from the yard and drop one into a whirlpool. At this, the lion would spring into action, seize the hapless ant in its jaws and deliver it a series of tiny body slams at the bottom of the pit. Then the victim was dragged under the sand and sucked dry. Some time later, the desiccated carcass was flicked out. Around each trap lay the wizened leftovers of many feedings which I deliberately left in the box for dramatic effect. After some weeks, however, the whirlpools began to disappear; soon all that was left of them were small shallow depressions. I dug around in the box and found that the ant lions had turned into cocoons. I had never seen cocoons like them before. They were like tiny, dirty tennis balls. Some days later, these quiescent spheres hatched like magic beans and delicate insects that looked like lacewings fluttered around my room eventually dying on the window sill.

My brother Tom, observing all this with an entrepreneurial eye, concocted the notion that with a thought-ful advertising strategy, *Myrmeleontidae* could be exploited commercially much in the way brine shrimp were peddled in comic books as "Adorable Sea Monkeys." His scheme was to call them "Sand Monsters." He envisioned marketing a small plastic, sand-filled replica of the Roman Coliseum where the blood sport of their feedings could be dramatized. Surely customers would clamor for such pets. "Heck, he said enthu-siastically, "we can even sell them the sand."

We wrote up sexy ads, designed in pencil the coli-seum, calculated the profits and for a time thought of little else. The only sticky point of the business was whether Sand Monsters could survive the shipping. Tom soon devised a test. One day he handed me an envelope.

Rawlston Schtunkenspiel
101 B East Chillypunch Avenue
Chicago, Illinois

"Who's Rawlston Schtunk...Schstunken....

"Schtunkenspiel. It isn't anybody. The address isn't anybody either. It's a test to see how these critters travel. The post office will stamp it with one of those fingers that says there isn't any such guy, and send it back. Then we can check to see how the ant lion did."

It was a brilliant idea. Soon ant lions enclosed in small plastic vials were boomeranging all over the country. Surpris-ingly, they fared pretty well. One Sand Monster was foolish enough to attempt an escape enroute to Connecticut and the postal machinery flattened him like a tiny, dry lion skin on the inside of the envelope, but aside from this, all but one of the participants made safe round trips, even in the summer heat. It was an ant lion with a round-trip ticket to New Jersey that showed up missing. Lost in the mail? Perhaps. Yet it remains my pet belief that providence actually directed this envelope to a mystified Rawlston Schtunkenspiel at his home on an oddly named Chillypunch Avenue, Union City, New Jersey.

Sadly, our best-laid plans floundered when it became apparent that we would not be able to maintain an adequate inventory to keep pace with the projected brisk demand. Our shipping tests and experimental "herd" had already exhausted the local supply, and lately, try as we might, we could collect only two or three specimens a day, hardly enough to turn a respectable profit. We began formulating plans to breed large numbers of sand monsters at home. We were determined to "wrangle" them ourselves. But we never got very far with it. Our remaining stock of one hundred had metamorphosed and were flying around the house like canaries.

Presently, Tom Jikek and I reach Blue Spring, finding it still in the shade and not quite as blue as I had remembered it. It will brighten up when the sun hits it. Much of the white sand on the bottom of the outlet is darkened by the sunken, worn down nubs of pinecones washed in from a side canyon. This time I am able to observe Blue Spring more closely. From a flat slab, directly above the main flow, bristle dense clusters of stalactites shaped like fat, hollow fangs. Gelatinous colonies of algae,nostoc nodules, a bright amber color in the sun, grow on the edges of the rocks where the water rushes over. Stepping over the rocks, I accidentally break one and a flap of it hangs down like a stubbed toe. I wonder how long it will take to heal over.

One hundred feet upstream I discover another source of the spring, a deep, underwater hole in the sand. At the bottom a smooth stone with a broad section of white quartz juts out glowing a ghostly blue in the sun; tiny whirlpools skim across the surface. I swim down and run my hand across the glassy stone. The water of Blue Spring remains a mild 68 degrees year round, but under the summer sun, it seems as cold as liquid snow. The Blue Spring area is a hot place in summer. Much of the day there is no shade at all unless you want to chase it around. We rig up plastic tarps against a cliff on the right bank and wait out the sun in sweltering blue shadows. Periodically we go down to the spring and plunge in, staying there until we're shivering. We are caught between hot and cold without much in between, but we are enjoying it just the same. There are tiny fish here, but the spring's high level of CO_2 restricts the larger fish—the channel cats, carp and humpback chubs, to the lower nine miles of the river. A spadefoot toad swims amid scummy rafts of algae along the bank.

At some point, Tom's brand-new aluminum walking stick, jammed into the sand by the river, has toppled in unnoticed and disappeared in the current. I have a similar trekking pole, one of those high tech, telescoping aluminum jobs with a tungsten tip. I'm not sure whether they float or not.

I've never tried floating one. I look through the clear water where it flows over boulders, thinking that the stick must have gotten hung up on the bottom, but I can't see it. Tom has already come to know the usefulness of a walking stick on a steep trail and, having given up his for lost, is searching around in the driftwood for a suitable replacement. In the meanwhile, I walk and wade far downstream in the late afternoon shadows, the alkaline water burning a little the scratches on my legs. To my surprise, I see something straining against a lone rock in the center of the shallow river. I wade across the sand to it. Sure enough, it's his stick floating on the water as buoyant as a gull.

Though the tracks of coyotes, mule deer and ringtails are in the mud, we have not seen much wildlife, but there is some evidence that wildlife sees us. On a little rise near the spring lies a wide, flat section of sand bordered with brush and scrubby trees. The eddy from a past flood has left a small delta of sticks and driftwood here. Mixed up in the sticks are old propane fuel canisters, motor oil bottles and a rusty one-gallon Coleman gas can washed in from Cameron. Lounging by the spring, we are startled to hear a loud, hollow, metallic bang which sounds every bit as if someone or something has kicked the metal can. I pull on my shoes and climb up to the flotsam. Nothing there. The layer of driftwood twigs doesn't allow for footprints. The old can is lying enigmatically against a driftwood log.

Our second night we camp behind a giant stone we have named Salvation Rock because it casts the only saving shade in late afternoon. When the sun finally disappears behind a notch on the canyon rim, the camp at Blue Spring becomes exceedingly comfortable. Before dark we cook up freeze-dried dinners and boil water for hot chocolate. While I have spoken in defense of Blue Spring's water, I will concede that it makes substandard coffee, and even worse green tea. Powdered Coffee Mate doesn't quite dissolve in it and remains suspended in clumpy particles in the cup. Even hot chocolate made from this water cannot reach its epicurean zenith unless rescued by adding half a can of evaporated milk. Just the same, it's good enough for us. It's a beautiful, comfortable evening. The sky turns black and the Big Dipper hangs upside down between the cliffs.

I watch the sky and as I drift off into sleep, my thoughts meander up canyon across the plateau and back into time. The remembrance flows upstream a hundred miles and more, and into the past twenty years and more, and I am living in a trailer along the edge of the Rio Puerco, the Little C's biggest tributary, another sand highway crossing the Painted Desert.

The Rio Puerco touches a tiny Arizona town named Sanders where once long ago I taught school for two years. Weekends I'd load up the pack, sling it on and walk out into the solitude of a red, ruddy landscape, and in my less cynical moments, hear a little of what Colin Fletcher called the rhythm of the rocks. The dry rivers cut through the strata of time and the music of the desert is in my ears and perhaps there are Arabian strains in it, for it brings to mind a desert strangely connected yet worlds away.

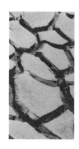

9

A Side Canyon

Almost 200 years ago the Swiss explorer, Johan Burckhardt, heard tales of an ancient lost city in what is now the southwestern part of Jordan, east of the village of Wadi Musa. The city is referred to as Sela in the Bible and was rumored to be hidden among a labyrinth of desert sandstone canyons accessible by a narrow ravine which wound its way between soaring cliffs. Bandits roamed the area and it was some time before Burckhardt was able to locate someone willing to take him there. Finally, an intrepid guide led him down a narrow chasm snaking through the red sandstone cliffs. The sandy path was barely ten feet wide. Suddenly, rounding a bend, Burckhardt was startled by the first and perhaps most astonishing of Petra's many temples, Khazneh el-Farun, the Treasury of the Pharaohs. Towering at the end of the chasm, it was an immense, ornate building, not erected from the ground up, but actually hewn from the living sandstone wall itself. In fact, this entire forgotten metropolis had been sculpted from the standing native stone of a vast Arabian canyonland. Burckardt had found his lost city, but its temples, tombs and treasuries, which offered so much promise, lay silent and empty.

The rusty sandstone cliffs soaring up from Black Creek Canyon's narrow stream reminded me a little of Petra, but their monuments, their temples and facades, were carved by nature, not men. Around no turn in the narrow red rock passage was there a treasury of kings. No sculpted columns held up friezes picturing horses and chariots. Had circumstances been different, pharaohs might have ruled here, kings of another fantastic Petra carved not into Arabian but American sandstone.

My first look into this cousin of the Gorge was many years ago with a friend named Joe Callahan, a guy who also worked at Puerco Middle School in Sanders. I remember him hanging by his fingers at the lip of a small cave in the rock, a big guy dangling twenty feet above the alluvium of a small side canyon. He had some odd habits. An hour earlier on the rim, he had stood before a gnarled old juniper with his arms spread, absorbing its cosmic energy, like a frog drinking through its skin.

"The Indians always did that," he said.

In his spare time, Joe was a Rosicrucian. Benjamin Franklin, he explained, was a Rosicrucian, and Benjamin Franklin had invented the lightning rod, daylight savings time, and bifocals, not to mention the Franklin stove. Naturally, Joe was anxious to place himself in such company. He needn't have explained it. The Rosicrucians were all right in my book if he was a member. In all the time I knew him, we never disagreed once about anything. Joe finished absorbing. Refreshed and fully charged, he continued trudging with me down the deep chasm of Black Creek Canyon.

But now Joe was hanging from a cliff. His tall body hung from the lip of a little sandstone pocket, a hole that looked as if it had been bored by an auger. Cosmic cave energy, no doubt, I thought. But this time he had an explanation that made sense, one that was full of wonder and truth, too. It was something I could buy into—a lot different from his notion about trees. It had a reasonable face on it.

Joe peered in the little hollow a moment and then dropped heavily. He swung back and forth by one hand and then the other, clinging to imperceptible cracks in the slick rock. He brachiated downwards like some great desert gibbon. Ten feet above bedrock his hold gave way and he crashed down. Then he explained what he had been doing up there.

He said that a thousand years ago, Indians had the habit of concealing things in such places. Nobody paid any attention to those little sandstone grottoes. Whatever was in that hole stayed there.

"Even if ten thousand people passed by, not a single one would look in that hole," he said.

"You're right," I said. "Who'd ever think to look?"

"They'd have no reason to," Joe said. "Besides, climbing up there's a hassle. So there's no telling what's hidden around here. Keep your eyes open for more likely places."

"What did you think would be in there?" I said.

"Whatever the Indian felt like hiding. A pot full of

beads, a stone ax, the skull of his father-in-law—any damn thing."

We walked on down the canyon.

"Whatever it is," he said, "it's bound to be something worth having."

He was right. It wouldn't matter. By the deliberate act of its concealment, and by virtue of its age, anything in that hole—pot, hatchet, skull, stove lid—would have taken on a mysterious significance. One would ask, "Why is this here? How long has it been hidden, and to what end?" and one would search for the meaning of it, and the mystery would persist, unsolvable. After a time the discoverer would put it out of his mind but he'd always carry it with him and in some odd moment maybe ten, twenty years later he would remember and wonder again.

Later Joe told me another story that was spun with the same gold thread of mystery. A friend of his had been hiking up on the red rock plateau. He wasn't far from highway I-40 nor was he far from a scattered community of hogans which had been occupied by Navajo sheepherders for a hundred years. The friend was walking across the dry red rock desert. After a while he sat down to rest and watch the sky. The clouds rolled by dreamily and the traveler fell asleep. An hour later he opened his eyes. He stood up and looked around. His vision was still hazy from sleep, but his eyes fell upon a wonder. There, next to him, on a flat-topped slab of sandstone where it had been waiting for 500 years, lay a heavy stone ax and with it, the vestiges of a wooden handle.

A stone ax left there by a passing Anasazi wanderer, a perfect creation of carved basalt.

The story was apocryphal, of course, but that didn't matter. What was important was that it *could* have been true.

"Why hadn't anyone seen it before?"

Joe answered with pleasure. "Nobody in 500 years had walked past that rock."

It was a perfect story, a story to which one could invent any of the particulars. For example, one could fashion it this way: An Indian boy on a quest had rested there, exhausted after a long journey. The boy had been bearing a ceremonial ax across the desert. But in a moment of carelessness he had left the holy object on the rock and continued on some miles without it. When he realized what had happened, he went back in an anguished effort to find it again. But that vast jumble of boulders defeated him. Rather than bear the public shame of having doomed the souls of his ancestors, for the ax was a sacred one, he threw himself off the cliffs of Black Creek Canyon.

The real story was probably more prosaic. More likely, another traveler discovered his error some miles after his rest stop and made a reasoned assessment. "Damnit. If I go back for that chopper now, I'll miss the whole freaking Corn Dance. Betty Lou (or whatever girls were called then) will probably run off with that guy from Wupatki." He thought about it a while. "Hell. It took me a good week to make that blasted ax, working all the time." He sat down on a rock not much different than the one upon which he had misplaced the tool. Again he thought hard, and after a couple of minutes he said, "Ah, screw it. I'll make another ax. But what an ass I am!" He walked off musing, his shoulders slumped dejectedly. "Nothing ever changes," he muttered. "It's always like this."

Black Creek Canyon runs through the Navajo Indian Reservation, south all the way down to a tourist trap called Fort Courage on Highway I-40. Here, its silty water, when it's running, is diverted under the blacktop through big culverts and joins the Rio Puerco on its way to the Little C. Fort Courage was an imitation cavalry fort inspired by the TV show *F Troop*. Inside the gift shop were glass cases of Indian jewelry, postcards, Kachina dolls, and gag souvenirs like cans of jackrabbit milk, or those little cylinders which when turned over make a soft, rubbery thump and then moo like a cow, or envelopes labeled *Rattlesnake Eggs* which startle you with a raspy buzz when you open them.

I once walked the canyon alone, all the way down to the Fort. The friendly proprietor of Fort Courage drove me up to where the canyon started. He was a healthy-looking, middle-aged guy who seemed to enjoy playing the role of tour guide. "I'm the only white man ever's been in there," he joked. He slowed the pickup where the road entered a copse of junipers on a hill. There were Indian ruins there, he said. He told me that he had once found fifty perfect arrowheads along where the grader piled up the dirt when the road was cut. After a while we reached a side canyon.

"Just walk on down there and you'll hit the main canyon," he said. "Follow it all the way down to Fort Courage. And let me know when you get back so's I don't have to come looking for you."

"I will. But if you're not in, my car's parked in front of your shop, that little blue Triumph. It should be gone by late tomorrow.

"Right."

I got out of the truck and heaved my pack out of the bed.

"Thanks a million."

"There's quicksand down there," he said out the window. "Don't worry about it, though. It's not the kind where you fall in and all that's left is your hat floating. But it's quicksand all right—bears too. I've shot a lot of bears down there. Haven't been in there for a while. Let me know if there's any bears down there."

"You eat them?"

"Sometimes I cut off a hind quarter. I don't like bear meat." He ground the gear shift on the column into reverse. "Toward the end you'll see ruins. Cliff dwellings. Kind of adhered to the rock."

There were bears, all right. Thousands of tracks wandered up and down the canyon. The quicksand mud was slick, with a bronze sheen to it. In it you could see where the big ones had dragged their paws as they walked. Some tracks plodded upstream, others down, and there were the small, frisky prints of cubs that here and there made little excursions as they followed the big tracks. Like the bears, I could walk right over the quicksand, but if I stopped it would begin to liquefy under my feet and I'd start to sink in. It couldn't have been very deep, but I avoided it anyway. It wasn't dangerous. Just messy.

Up over the red rock rim of the canyon, I occasionally heard the sound of bells clanking. Goats. Looking up, I could see the downy cotton of airborne seeds in the wind lit like sparks in the bright sun. The canyon was narrow and between its walls were strewn boulders and logs and other debris. In the middle of the streambed I came upon the remains of a car, a red compact, its make rendered indecipherable by the flash flood that had trundled it here from miles upstream. It was tangled up with driftwood and inside, river stones cemented by sand formed a solid matrix.

How many miles to Fort Courage? I hadn't worked out the mileage. I had no map and this was fine planning, for the landscape that opened up to me would be new and unexpected and undiscovered. I thought a little about the bears, though. The tracks were everywhere and the channel of the canyon so narrow I was sure to surprise one. I looked at the smaller tracks and imagined turning a corner and coming upon a cub and mother, never a good idea.

I walked across rock and gravel and through trees and shade. Once, next to a boulder of a type of pockmarked basalt geologists call scoria, I found an old lard can. It had been chewed by bears. Their teeth had punched right through the heavy steel can. It was almost as if it had been shot full of holes by someone plinking with a .22. Thinking back, I can't really say I was worried much. After all, who ever really got eaten by a bear?

There were curious little teepees in the canyon. They were old things constructed of wood and bark and stood about three feet tall. I came across four or five of them where they were weathering away under trees or at the base of the cliffs. Aside from the mangled car, the lard can, and the traces of ancient dwellings high on the cliffs, these were the only man-made objects in the canyon. I still have no idea what they were. But there are plenty of mysteries in the desert. Just that same month Joe and I had come across a real human skeleton stretched out under an overhang near Burnt Water. It had been there a while and the bones almost entirely picked clean. One of the teeth fell out when I lifted the skull. A traditional Navajo burial? We never found out. I wandered all day down Black Creek Canyon, past pools of water and patchy green meadows. Once I scared up some cows.

Late in the day I made my camp next to a fallen obelisk of pink sandstone. I propped my pack up with a piece of driftwood and built a fire in the shade of the afternoon. The feet of birds had scattered indecipherable cuneiforms in the sand. On the near cliff wall, an ancient sandstone crag towered into the sky like a colossus, and with the changing light, shadows played on the rocks, giving expression to what seemed like stolid Egyptian faces. Present and past mingle companionably in such a setting. My fire could have been awaiting any one of a thousand nights.

As the sky darkened, I finished a supper of sardines and crackers and listened to the descending notes of canyon wrens. I melted the sardine can in the fire, turning it with a stick until the aluminum glowed red, turned to paper, and disappeared in the orange flames. The fire died down. In the dark I removed from my pack a soot-blackened can into which I sloshed water from my old army canteen. I positioned the can over the fiery cubes of alligator juniper. When the water was boiling nicely, I added two pouches of Swiss Miss chocolate powder and stirred it with a stick, and when it had cooled enough, I used my bandanna as a potholder and drank the hot chocolate right from the can.

The coals gave off an orange glow. Then the moon broke over the cliffs like a Pharos in the east and Orion cartwheeled across the sky. Somewhere nearby, a gang of coyotes started up and raised hell for a whole hour. I celebrated with them—downed two canned gin martinis (no Boy Scout was ever better prepared) and beneath silent, sandstone sphinxes, I fell into a sodden sleep.

I slept shivering under a blue Mexican blanket, one with a design of blackbirds flying across it. I might just as well not have had a blanket for all the good that one did me. I'd lugged that blanket in this same backpack, riding on trains and buses, all the way from the town of San Andreas south of Mexico City where my brother Jeff had given it to me. He was living in a house in the cornfields near the Great Pyramid of Cholula, by volume the largest man-made structure in the world. I remember wandering all day along the rows of corn searching for, and sometimes finding, small prehistoric faces made out of stone and clay left by the Indians who had built the pyramid. The natives called them caritas, little faces. I still have them.

In the morning I made instant coffee flavored by last night's leftover chocolate. Then I smashed up the martini cans with a stone, loaded up my old green pack, and continued on. Only one night in the canyon and I was already walking in a dream. The soothing creak of the pack and the crunch of footsteps over gravel and sand lulled me. Hiking can be a kind of somnambulism where thoughts become random and mixed and take odd turns the way bats fly. I was remembering the long cold night and the familiar feeling a deer mouse left when he hopped across my back in the dark.

I was awakened by a vague consciousness of noises ahead. I stopped and listened. Something was scratching around in the brush down canyon. A bear? I kept walking. What else could I do? A minute later I rounded a bend and there he was, the big black bear I'd been expecting, standing sure-footed on a fan of dry, rocky talus looking down at me. The sun glared off his back a coppery red. I expected him to run, but he just glowered. This Kentucky standoff didn't last long. I cut across the canyon floor and climbed up a little hill where I could find a suitable climbing tree. I cursed when I realized that in the tall scrub I had lost sight of the bear. Then I heard rocks rasping down the talus and dirt flying and sticks getting broken. I ran around the trees in a mad, suicidal impulse to meet him head on.

But he wasn't after me. He was running away, tearing across the talus, dislodging prickly pear cactus and pale green yucca. I whacked my walking stick on a rock and he doubled his speed. He ran with terror, fearing perhaps a bullet from the trigger-happy proprietor of Fort Courage—imagining his hind quarter served up unenthusiastically by a guy who didn't even like bear meat.

A few miles downstream deep, sand-bottomed pools had gathered in the stone. The sun was high and it was hot now. I stripped off my pack and everything else and plunged in. Later I lay on the smooth slabs of stone drying in the sun with the smell of the water and rocks around me. Far up on the red cliff wall was a line of Joe's secret caves. I wondered how deep they were and if any of them held treasure. A tiny Anna's Hummingbird whirled out of nowhere to examine a multicolored bandanna knotted to the pack frame. Its red throat gleamed like foil in the hot sun. Then it took off disdainfully, scrawling a loop like the end of a big shot's signature. It was getting late. I got dressed and continued walking. The canyon had begun to flatten and widen now. I was nearing the end.

Soon I found the cliff dwellings. They clung to the rock as if plastered there by mud daubers. Broad slabs of pottery, decorated with jagged geometric forms, lay high up on the ruins. The site had never been excavated. The whole structure was dried and crumbling. Anyone climbing up to where there once had been doors and rooms and hearths would bring down a lethal landslide of prehistoric rubble.

By late afternoon the canyon spread out into a delta whose waters led to the Rio Puerco, to the Little Colorado, to the Colorado, and eventually to the Sea of Cortez. Ravens croaked overhead. One last tall cliff remained. High up on the red rock was a hole, an impression so dark it might have been painted with a dab of black ink. These holes, often referred to as tafoni, are characteristic of desert regions. In wetter climes, rock surfaces are more uniformly moist than in the desert where a recessed area on a cliff may weather far faster than the bone-dry exterior. The result is desert windows, arches, bridges and holes such as this.

Against the blue sky from the top of the canyon, swirls of little white leaves, perhaps the dry petals of primroses, fluttered down. I watched for a moment as their whirling circles descended. Then I slung my pack off. It was hard climbing. Following Joe's example, I clung to the rock face until I gripped the edge of the hole. It was a small opening. My pack couldn't have fit in it. I chinned myself up and looked in.

Back at Fort Courage I told the proprietor about the bears. Too late I realized he'd probably head up there and blast the bear population down so far that it might never bound back again. I told him about the mysterious teepees and the wrecked car and the lard can and the ruins. I didn't tell him about the hole in the rock because there was nothing to tell—it was empty. It might have contained something once, but maybe its treasures had been plundered in antiquity like the temples of Petra. All it contained were a few flakes of the papery petals of desert primroses swirling in eddies of wind. Nothing else was in there, and in a thousand years there won't be anything else in there either. Only now, so many years later, does it occur to me that I could have left something in that little grotto—my Kamp King pocketknife whose stainless steel blades would turn bronze with age. Or better yet, the beat-up copy of *Desert Solitaire* I carried in my pack, which would wither over the centuries like the Dead Sea Scrolls. But Black Creek Canyon was never a Petra or meant to be. Nobody will ever look in that hole again, and if they ever did, they'd find no mystery, just primroses.

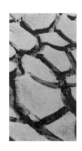

10

Horse Trail Morning
May 30, 2002

I awake in the gray light and listen to the spring. It is a while before I remember last night's reverie and reflect that I have slept on what was once Black Creek sand. There is another thing I ponder, and that is a theme of the story—the thesis that what was once litter in time becomes artifact: the coffee cans and old lanterns left by miners, the old copper whiskey still abandoned by moonshiners of a colorful age, the garbage of a midden heap, all tell the story of life in times long past. The trash around such Grand Canyon ruins as Beamer's Cabin near the confluence is now protected under the American Antiquities Act. The rusty cans and broken bottles, once ordinary expressions of life, have been reborn the way old metaphors long disused can become new again. I suppose it isn't a very original conjecture. Wasn't it Andy Warhol who boxed the contents of his office wastebaskets for prosperity? Still, nothing is more interesting than the relics of the past, particularly when you can lift them and think.

Browsing on the Internet recently, I found in the Grand Canyon Hiker's E-mail Group, a vignette which followed along the lines of this motif. It recounted a surprising discovery near remote Fossil Bay in the Grand Canyon. Jammed into a sandstone crevice was a sealed, five-gallon can. Age had stained the exposed metal to match the hue of the adjacent rocks, but the interior was still bright and silvery. Inside it, hiker Jim Ohlman discovered a small white and orange parachute, plastic bags containing coffee and sugar, a pair of sunglasses and a note:

> *"To finder (especially Harvey Butchart)—If you have time and energy to pack this parachute out to "Tex" Wright of Wright Airflight, Municipal Airport, Flagstaff, he will probably be grateful. Tell him it was the one used to drop food to Colin Fletcher near here.*
> *4/27/63.*
> *(Harvey: your sunglasses underneath chute—and some odds and ends) Colin Fletcher, 5/3/63"*

Fletcher had relied on several caches including two dropped to him from planes during his Grand Canyon through hike, the first continuous walk through the entire length of the park. His journal, of course, became the classic GC book *The Man Who Walked Through Time*. I always wondered if Fletcher had returned to the canyon to tidy up those caches. But what Fletcher left was not litter, not anymore anyway. It was a relic of Grand Canyon history.

Interestingly enough, Fletcher himself found this same fascination with relics and the stories behind them. While hiking in a remote section of Nevada in 1965, he discovered a cave containing the abandoned remains of a man's solitary life. Fletcher was immediately intrigued. Who was this man and how had he come to live in this secret, desert cave?

With a persistence few others could muster, Fletcher began a years-long effort to ferret out and study the clues: a scrap of a 1916 newspaper, an empty trunk, old spent cartridges, a hand-made chair. The resulting book, *The Man from the Cave*, unfolds like a detective story. Fletcher has often likened walking in the wilderness to an exercise of self discovery, and his book seems to follow in this vein. His search led, strangely, somehow inevitably, to a man who was a disquieting silhouette of himself.

Here in the Gorge there is rarely a sign of man. The Gorge was never a friendly place for living. There are no ruins, no cliff dwellings, at least any I know of, until the river reaches the Grand Canyon and Beamer's Cabin.

11

Up Blue Spring Trail
May 30, 2002

There is danger in a summer desert and it is difficult to anticipate it. Danger is by nature unpredictable. The best you can do is follow the rules and use what you know to keep small circumstances from adding up to trouble. This, of course, goes against the grain of human nature. Since I have a little experience hiking in the desert, Tom Jilek is willing to go along with my itinerary, trusting me to keep us out of trouble.

Early in the morning we head upstream a few hundred feet to the foot of the Blue Spring Trail. This little track ends above the left bank of the river where enormous cubes of fallen rock lie jumbled in the water. The climb up to the trail is easy and once on it, we find the path friendly and simple to follow. Our intentions are a bit unfocused. Neither of us is very ambitious this morning. Our legs are still aching a bit from the downhill hiking on Horse Trail. I'm figuring we'll go up a ways, have a look around and come back. But as our muscles become accustomed to the climbing, we grow inspired and continue along until we are climbing hand over hand up stone chimneys to cairns perched high above. I know that the most ghastly parts of Blue Spring Trail are in the Kaibab Limestone near the very summit. Bill Orman wrote to me before the trip: "At the top there is a short exposed section that traverses a ledge to a cairn on a point and it's definitely not for everybody. When I first saw it I was solo with a daypack and I turned around."

But it's not the possibility of falling that worries me now. The canyon is cool and shady, but as I watch the sunlight sliding up the cliff, I feel a tinge of nervousness. "How much water have you got?" Tom opens his day pack and pulls out a half-full Platypus bottle of purple, grape-flavored spring water. One quart. I'm not carrying much more myself.

"Hell," I said. "I know better than this. We should have more water. I wasn't figuring we'd go this far." I look up the steep edifice of limestone. We are almost to the top. "Let's go up just a little bit more check out the hairy spots and then get back before Old Yellow Face fries us."

We keep climbing. Though we have enough water to reach the river, I am aware that there isn't much margin for error. And there is something I haven't factored into the scenario. Unlike most trails, Blue Spring is a faster climb up than down. It's easier and quicker to ascend the cliffs than to pick your way down. Those experienced with the route allow two hours for strong hikers to reach the rim and twice that to descend to the river. Anyone walking with a big backpack, for example, would be smart to rope it down in places. It isn't much faster with a day pack. My instincts tell me that we could be walking into a trap.

After a while we come to a place I'm not in the least bit interested in crossing. Tom Jilek has also had a bellyful of it. We've gotten our money's worth. Time to turn around. We are surprised, and a little disturbed, however, to find that places that had been easy climbs coming up are tricky and scary going down. Looking over the ledges makes me almost dizzy, and one place, not a big drop at all, shakes me. I chicken out and crab back up the rock. I find another way and crunch down into a rubbly little gulch, still high up the canyon. The sun has climbed the talus. Its rays are pretty sharp, but we have begun to make some progress. Then fortune throws us a little scare. Following the cairns, we come to a drop-off we can't descend. We don't remember this place at all. There is a labyrinth of courses down the Blue Spring Trail, each branch guided by a separate series of rock markers. Why cairns lead here we can't imagine. We aren't exactly lost, but we're definitely off our route. A little worry creeps into my head.

"Well, what now?" Tom says.

I think a minute. "We'll have to go back to a place we remember for sure and relocate our way down. Remember that spot where we had to scrape our bellies climbing over that flat-topped boulder? That's just a little way uphill. We aren't far off."

We reach the belly-scraping rock and I am relieved to see on the left, far down on a broad sloping talus, another flat, red rock with a familiar cairn of blocks on it. "There's our route." We pick our way down to it and after a few short climbs and a traverse down a steep wash, we reach the defined section of trail where we stride along in the scalding sun all the way to the little cliff above the river. Here, in a patch of shadow, we drink our last swallows of water before descending to the stream bed. We boulder hop to the spring and plunge into the chilly water.

I don't suppose we were ever in any real danger, but we were close enough. Rule number one is always water. Any desert hike in summer, even a short one, requires a gallon, period. Another rule is to know your plans. We broke that one by starting up the trail without any clear intentions, and the general ambition we had, that of looking around a little, we changed and made bigger. But our water supply had not changed to match it. The complications of delays on the downhill return and getting off track pushed the time and water equation more than was comfortable. Another surprise or two on the trail might have gone poorly for us.

12

Out The Horse Trail
May 30-31, 2002

After waiting out the afternoon sun, we pack up and march up to camp number one just down from the Horse Trail and the next morning we reach the foot of the Horse where piles of sticks and rocks on a large river boulder mark the entrance. To be doubly certain of the spot, we had been careful to memorize the unusual shape of the towering butte here, for the canyon through which the Horse Trail ascends is not at all obvious from the riverbed. Until you climb up over the first overhang, it is not overly apparent that there is a side canyon here at all.

It is early, but the way up is hot and sweaty nevertheless and the air is uncommonly still. When we arrive at the final scree slope leading to the big drop-off, it is drenched in sunlight, but at the top of the rise lies the overhang with its promise of shade. Tom strides ahead and waits patiently in the cool shadows for his slower companion. A first timer, he has proved to be an excellent hiker, with a positive, enthusiastic attitude and no big ego. Moreover, he stoically endures my nonstop blabbering.

From here it's an easy walk out, particularly since we

find the main trail which we missed on our descent. Coming in, we had walked the wash down to the drop-off, following cairns left by other off-route visitors, unaware of the fast, smart little path on the north side of the drainage. The big, white, shiny Chevy is waiting untouched where we left it. Under the fiery sun a sweeping landscape of red weathering rock and small, sandy buttes surrounds us, receding into the distance. It's a fine, memorable day. As it turns out, it's more memorable than we know. Harvey Butchart has died. He was ninety-five.

13
Little Colorado Day Five
Blue Pool

Jeff awakens with a case of hammertoe. I don't know exactly what hammertoe is, but he definitely has it and I definitely don't want it. He spends a long time doctoring the hammertoe. He uses tape and Band Aids and plastic and foam to treat the hammertoe. A good portion of the symptoms of hammertoe are verbal. As he treats his hammertoe, Jeff utters oaths of the hottest kind seasoned effusively with blasphemous biblical allusions. Believe me, you do not want to hike in the Gorge if you have hammertoe. Jeff, an expert on the minutia of any subject, mutters something about phalangeal joints. I have not yet bothered to research the particulars of the condition, but I surmise that it is something that makes your toe feel as if it has been hit by a hammer.

I wait until I judge it is safe to speak. "Are you ready yet?"

He looks up with red rimmed eyes, nods, and bravely shoulders his pack.

As we walk, the Gorge seems to brighten. Scores of rushing falls cascade over travertine terraces into shockingly blue pools. The color of the water has become almost unnatural, as if the river were running with sky blue paint. At times the Little C seems to take on its own luminescence as if it were charged with neon. Viewing Jeff's snapshots, his Texas friends are later to accuse him of doctoring the negatives. The shallows here are white-bottomed, coated with thick sediment. Squeezed in the hand, the mud is as smooth and white as porcelain clay. This, along with the dissolved carbonates in the water, combines with the glaring sun to reflect the blue end of the spectrum. We pass more springs, where percolating water creates streamlets connecting marshy patches on the right bank. We find concretions of travertine shaped like odd bottles of blown glass or like piles of cannon balls soldered together by rust. Once we pass through a salt cave.

The symptoms of hammertoe have abated in Jeff and we pick our way slowly along the bank and wade or float through the river when we must. Stands of green cattails grow out of the white sand on the shore, lovely to the eye but murder to get through. It becomes more and more apparent why the Gorge is so rarely trekked and why so few people have seen these sights. The going is rough. Quicksand is a continual annoyance. More than once I find myself stuck nearly to the waist in two feet of water, lying half on the shore with the heavy pack on my back. The mud seems to suck like the devil and it's exhausting to drag myself out of it. Wrenching his walking stick free from the mud, Jeff finds that the rubber tip has been sucked clean off.

On the left bank we find our worst horrors. Detouring around the stream we must bushwhack through skin-ripping mesquite and catclaw forests. The inner tube tied neatly on Jeff's pack is soon torn up and spills down his back in lime-green shreds. Mine becomes a deflated candy apple a few minutes later. We'll have to do without them.

Now we climb high up on the talus where a massive flash flood has left in its passing a huge bundle of driftwood. We have often stopped to marvel at such places. These heaps of wood, along with prehistoric gray logs balanced on boulders high above the river, tell of unimaginable floods. Crossing this bridge of sticks, I lose my balance and attempt to regain it with my trekking pole. The sharp-tipped pole pokes right through the wood which offers no more resistance than shredded wheat. I crash down on my face. At the last moment the pole bangs into rock. My REI trekking poles have spring mechanisms designed to give a little when you use them. The object of this feature is to reduce stress on the arms, to avoid what might result in a kind of hammertoe of the elbow, I suppose. In any case, the spring-loaded pole vaults over my shoulder and falls clattering on the rocks below. When I climb down to retrieve it, I find that the bottom section of the pole is badly bent. I try to straighten it over my knee and after considerable effort I succeed in breaking it right in half.

We are not making much progress in this section of the Gorge, a half a mile an hour at best, but we continue to discover wonderful things: a travertine dam where the water has found a shortcut under the stone and boils up like a cold white haystack; stretches of bubbling sands; a diving place overlooking a deep opaque swimming hole the color of blue sidewalk chalk. Black channel cats rise to the surface and swirl in the current. Two dead swifts float in a pool. We thread our way through willowy stands of new tamarisks parting the feathery leaves as we go, and from the water and the silt and the thin, blossoming tammies there arises, as always, a smell like pepper. And then something even more miraculous. In the brackish current I find adhered to the travertine, rubbery forms like ocean sponges which seem to be breathing through little holes, nostoc nodules, a form of bluegreen algae.

We camp at the shore of a blue pool where gold carp glide over a submerged hill of white sand in the bright sun. There is a gentle current here meandering around a colossal block of yellow sandstone rising out of the deepest part.

14
Little Colorado Day Six
Camp Beamer

We have begun to settle into the routine of living outdoors and start to feel that we could live comfortably like this forever. But six days have had an effect. I have noticed that in writing in my notebook the words come sluggishly and spelling is more difficult than usual. There is another thing that both of us have noticed—a mysterious third presence. Leaving a camp or a rest spot in the shade, both of us have found ourselves turning more than once somehow expecting to see this "other" and then realizing there are only two of us. I pause at times as if to wait. I look over my shoulder only to see an empty, lonely canyon. It's a spooky feeling. Were we superstitious we would no doubt ascribe this to an actual presence—Castaneda's Mescalito, perhaps, or Kokopelli or, even worse—a malevolent Hopi Two Heart. It is only now that I realize who it is. It is our brother Tom. He had shuttled us from the head of the Tanner Trail, where we had parked my Toyota wagon, to Cameron, but he had opted not to hike the Gorge. Now as the beauty of the canyon becomes greater, along with the greatness of our adventure, we are looking for him.

We pass Big Canyon and then Salt Trail Canyon, tributaries entering on the right. We can't know it but we are just ahead of a tragedy. Already this summer a new Grand Canyon book entitled *Over the Edge: Death in Grand Canyon* has been published by Michael P. Ghiglieri and Thomas M. Myers. It is a chronicle of disasters in the Park which records the deaths of hikers, sightseers, and rafters from falls, drownings, air crashes, suicides, murders, flash floods and environmental factors. While the book serves to satisfy the morbid curiosity of any reader, it also describes many of the insidious circumstances which have so often added up to fatality and offers many heads-ups to future canyoneers. The coming tragedy here in the Gorge will no doubt be included in a future edition.

The event is to happen just up Big Canyon where noted Flagstaff photographer George Mancuso and his companion Linda Brehmer will hike to view a little-known canyon site. They will enter the Gorge by way of the primitive Salt Trail in Salt Trail Canyon just downstream of Big Canyon. Mancuso will be embarking on another of many photographic projects below the rim, for he specialized in inner canyon photography. Marketing postcards of his images has become a successful business. Mancuso is well-known at the Canyon and regarded as a canyoneer of the first degree. Years of work in the studio have earned him the respect of the photography crowd as well. It has been his intention to continue the tradition of Canyon photography first embarked upon by the famous Kolb Brothers almost a century ago. A regular fixture in the park, he is known to the river rafters who have grown to expect seeing him near the Little Colorado confluence.

When Brehmer and Mancuso are reported ten days overdue, no one is overly concerned. Mancuso has a reputation for showing up late. Only last year he turned up missing and a search was launched. As it turned out, he had embarked on an impromptu river trip, having hitched a ride with a rafting party. This did not endear him to the Park Service. Nor had his habit of hiking without a permit. Still, the Park will send a helicopter to the Gorge where Mancuso and Brehmer's tidy camp is found at the junction of Salt Canyon and the Gorge. The two hikers are not there. Most ominous are the signs of recent flash flooding. Indeed, the search proceeds at a cautious pace because of the monsoon weather.

At the camp, Brehmer's notebook indicates that the pair has gone upstream to Big Canyon to see Emerald Pool. When searchers reach the mouth of the side canyon, they find it choked with the debris from a recent flood and they proceed up the wash with dread. It is not difficult to guess what has become of the two hikers. Near the green pool beneath a travertine fall, they find Brehmer's body. A few days later, Mancuso's will be located far downstream near the confluence.

Surprisingly, *Over the Edge* documented only six flash flood deaths at the time of its release. The low number seems in part the product of dumb luck, for the book recounts numerous close calls where scores of individuals have come literally inches from being swept away. In one case a helicopter pilot in Havasu Canyon saved multiple lives by rushing downstream signaling an urgent warning just ahead of a six-foot wall of water. But there will be no one to warn Brehmer and Mancuso and for all his experience and expertise, Mancuso, like anyone in the canyon, is not immune to happenstance. It will be speculated that the soaring cliffs blocked the view of localized thunderheads to the east over the Painted Desert.

A day or two after I read of the tragedy, I will remember with a certain shock, the comfortable-looking hiker Jeff and I met at the foot of the Tanner Trail years before, the one from Flagstaff who said he made postcards of the Grand Canyon.

Not far beyond Salt Trail Canyon, we come across a landmark I have been looking forward to visiting, The Hopi Sipapu, or vagina pot. It is here, according to Hopi religion, that the first humans were born into the world, a kind of Eden. The Sipapu is a brown, ponderous travertine mound shaped like a gigantic serving of flan. Barefoot, I wade the river and climb a faint path to the top where I find a gaping undercut hole in the center. Eight feet down lies a pool of emerald-green water with an orange, flame skimmer dragonfly floating dead on the surface. Big bubbles of CO_2 wriggle up and sizzle. This is a holy place and out of respect we have resolved to forego swearing until we are well away and are astonished to find how easily this can be accomplished with a little concentration.

Years ago, I had read *Sun Chief,* the 1937 autobiography of Hopi, Don Talayesva. In the account he tells of a pilgrimage he made as a teenager in 1912 with his father and another man into the Grand Canyon to gather salt. The three entered the Little Colorado River Gorge via Salt Trail Canyon just upriver from the Sipapu. Their approach to the Salt Trail was marked by two sacred geologic formations. One was the figure of the Salt Woman, an entity with whom, tradition dictated, the three men must simulate copulation, the rock featuring a serviceable orifice. "This is not a 'dirty trick' as the Christians have called it," Talayesva related, "...neither is it the worship of a stone image, for we know that the Salt Woman is a living goddess, and that intercourse with her means life."

Also on the route stood the petrified remains of one of the Hopi War Twins, a spirit who turned himself into a jagged stone to mark the way. From here Talayesva looked for the first time into the Gorge.

"I looked into the canyon which seemed miles deep, and saw the Little Colorado River shining from the bottom. I was frightened and wondered if we would ever return in safety."

On the rough climb down, the men passed more places of significance where offerings were left: The Nose Scraping Place, the Chicken Shrine, where pictures of chickens were drawn in red ochre by the War Twins, and the cave shrine of a god named Masau'u. After reaching the bed of the Gorge and drinking the sacred blue water, Don Talayesva and his fellow worshippers hiked downriver to visit the Sipapu. The teenager was offended to see that some "ignorant, foolhardy Whites" had jammed two long poles into the sacred spring.

Here the three Hopis left offerings of feathers and corn meal, collected clay, and then trekked to the junction of the Little Colorado and Colorado rivers. They walked in reverence and with a certain amount of fear, always careful not to look too closely at things or to offend the spirits in any way, for they knew that their journey was one of consequence, a pilgrimage potent enough to bring rain to their land and to assure them a happy life and a peaceful old age.

It had been a magical experience for the young Hopi, one that affirmed his belief in his religion and his growing conviction that contrary to what the white man had taught him in the government schools, his people played a unique and important part in the world. From the Sipapu, the three continued on to where the two rivers joined and then downstream on cliffs above the Colorado River.

Some miles from the confluence along the south side of the Colorado stands the first War Twin's brother, also metamorphosed. The second twin exists in the form of a unique knob of stone protruding from the bed of an arroyo. The men knotted their rope around the chest of this benignant second twin and slid down to mine the shallow caverns. Here white straws of salt hung from the ceilings of grottos but the best chunks, Talayesva was instructed, needed to be dug up from where they lay hidden under the sand.

In one cave, bitter medicine dripped from a stalactite of salt into a natural cup atop a truncated cone of limestone. Talayesva was astonished to see submerged in this "medicine bowl" small stone figurines in the shape of mountain lions.

His father explained to him that anyone who wished could make out of bread dough the likeness of an animal and place it in the brine. After a year, the spirit gods will have turned the figure to stone and one could return to find a calcified effigy.

Talayesva's journey was a successful one. According to his account, the three men departed the Gorge carrying 180 pounds of salt, 60 pounds apiece. Some of this they left as an offering to the Salt Woman on the plateau. But the weight of salt was not the measure of their success. When they arrived in Oraibi, Talayesva wrote:

> "We sprinkled more meal and my father said, 'Well, at last we are back, bringing the Cloud God with us. With happy hearts we will enter our homes'. Then the Cloud People, who had trailed us from the sacred river, poured rain upon our crops—a true miracle."

I visited the Sipapu much in the way a tourist might visit an historic cathedral. There was a moment when it entered my head that I was intruding. Then I remembered what Don Talayesva said about the Whites who had defiled the spring with the poles: "Those profane fellows had desecrated the sacred spot where our ancestors—*and theirs*—emerged from the underworld. It was a great disgrace." The Sipapu is not just the birthplace of the Hopis, but of all humanity. Talayesva's inclusiveness not only makes me feel a little less unwelcome but it underlines the importance the tribe placed in their religion. The Hopi practice not just a little religion, but one as super eminent as any of the big, name-brand faiths. The fizzing water of this beguiling spring tells a creation story every bit equal to the mud and rib bone version.

I would have liked very much to visit the Hopi salt mines if only to see the second War Twin and the medicine bowl atop the travertine stalagmite in the cave. But the ordinance regarding the Hopi salt mines has been specific for years. They are off limits. This dictum is essential. Not only is this area more fragile than the Sipapu, but its access is not buffered by a hard thirteen mile round trip slog from the Colorado. The Hopi salt is accessible by boats from the river. With twenty thousand river runners passing each year, the rule has helped protect the site.

Nevertheless, there have been a handful of Anglos who have visited the salt caves and to one the Hopis owe a debt. Not long after Talayesva's journey, the traditional Hopi pilgrimages were discontinued. While the Sipapu remained sacred, the knowledge of the way to the salt mines was lost. Young Hopis who attempted to renew the pilgrimages could not locate them. Fortunately, in the late 1950s Harvey Butchart became fascinated with the story of the lost salt and set out to rediscover it using Talayesva's narrative as a guide. A knotty point of Talayesva's account was that it neglected to mention whether the source was upriver or down. A river runner acquaintance of Butchart's, Dock Marston, believed he had found the site some miles upstream from the mouth of the Little C. But an aspect of Marston's location did not jibe with Talayesva's description. The salt deposits Marston reported were accessible by simply walking along the shore. Since the mine described in Talayesva's book required a rope descent, Butchart dismissed Marston's theory and searched downstream, eventually finding the place below the Beamer Trail just as the Hopi had remembered it. Butchart was impressed by the War Twin above the salt, calling it

> "...the most peculiar example of erosion of bedrock I have ever seen in the bed of a wash. It stands out like a saddle horn a foot in diameter, and it is located exactly where you need to fasten a rope for the shortest rappel."

15

The Salt Trail
November 22, 2002

My brother Tom and I stand on a hill and look down into Salt Trail Canyon just downstream of Bekihatso Wash and see as Don Talayesva did almost a century before, the Little Colorado "shining from the bottom." This is an obvious passage to the river because from the rim you can see far in the distance below, radiant in the sunshine, the beckoning blue water and rushing white falls. Getting here has been something of a business. The route across the Reservation to the trailhead begins north of the Tuba City cutoff, already close to the middle of nowhere, and then travels on dirt roads over twenty-five miles of red rock and open space. A canyoneer has mailed me a detailed road log. But it has been a year or so since he has visited Salt Trail Canyon and he does not know that a small landmark marking a crucial turn, a red metal sign with a number, is no longer there.

On our way here, we have chosen a small side road, and though it was the wrong one, we eventually connect to the correct path and picked up our friend's other carefully recorded landmarks: three beat up hogans on the left, a small cluster of whitish stones, the round rock foundation of an ancient hogan. Soon we pass a flock of sheep and a pack of sheep dogs tears across the desert to intercept us. A wildly woolly black and white, tassel-eared dog barks angrily at the door. Tom guns the engine but the fast, protective dogs follow a quarter of a mile before they are satisfied that the sheep are safe. I see them in the rearview mirror, no longer running, but still barking and sneezing and licking their noses in the cold air.

Now as we look into the canyon, a bright red Chevy pickup descends a hill and parks beside us. We chat for a while with the driver, a Navajo hired to watch the sheep. He knows quite a bit about the canyon. He tells us that when he was young he once descended Salt Trail Canyon and trekked all the way to the confluence and exited out Beamer and Tanner. He offers few details of the trip except that he had lost his wallet somewhere in the Gorge and that it was returned months later by ichthyologists studying the Little C's fish.

"It's very steep in there," he says, and points to a small cairn marking a faint trail into the wash above the drainage. "You start there and then go down to where it drops in. It's very steep."

"You still go in there sometimes?"

He laughs. "I'm not in condition anymore."

Talking with him is exceedingly pleasant. Right away I recognize the type. Typical of Navajos, he has a soft Indian accent and a modest manner which might have be mistaken for innocence but which is really only civility.

Tom and I drag our packs out of the truck bed. They

are heavy. We are packed for a winter hike. We'd spent an icy night near Flagstaff where the temperature had fallen to the low twenties and I don't know how much warmer it will be as we descend into the Canyon. We are loaded with down coats, gloves, sweaters, wool caps, long fleece pants and heavy sub-zero sleeping bags. Accustomed as I am to hiking in the heat, it is difficult to put aside the urge to pack a lot of water. We carry a gallon each.

The trail leads down between two tall cairns which stand like sentinels to the Gates of Mordor. From here the route fairly plunges over the edge. While hiking the Horse Trail with a big pack is challenging, and the Blue Spring Trail perilous, the Salt Trail is, well, medium dangerous, at least for us. There are few places to make a straight-air fall, but there are plenty of spots to stumble and break every bone in your body. For the hardcore canyoneer, the passage may seem a dreamboat with just enough challenge to make it interesting. For my brother and me, however, it's different. With the heavy packs balanced on our backs, working down the chute of jumbled yellow blocks is difficult and scary. Tom, in particular, is at a disadvantage. Although he's a strong hiker, he's not all that fond of it; he has only come along because he wanted to look at birds. Those heavy, three-hundred-dollar Swift Audubon binoculars swinging from a strap around his neck aren't helping much. Despite my warnings of what the terrain might be like, he had still imagined walking upright on something resembling a trail. In addition to this, he has ignored my advice and stuffed into his pack many glass bottles of Redhook beer. He has decanted a pint of another specialty brew into a plastic canteen stuffed into a side pocket. The cap is loose. A hoppy aroma follows in his wake. Worst of all, he is a studied doomsayer. At every precipice he imagines a fall and supplies with many adjectives the details of shocking compound fractures. If I point out an interesting rock, he is apt to make dark allusions to its precarious position and comment on the damage such a heavy object would do if it were to trundle over your skull. In the distant roaring of jets, he imagines approaching flash floods and often pauses to evoke appalling visions. All this crepe hanging fills me with dread. My mind is laden with morbid thoughts of tragedy and catastrophe.

Granted, he isn't enjoying my company much either. My pedagogical lectures on the use of a walking stick are wearing him down. I can't help it. He considers the stick an inconvenience, just something else to carry or trip over. When I express my exasperation at his refusal to be instructed, he suggests a use for the stick not mentioned in the REI brochure.

There is also the matter of his shoes. Tom doesn't have any heavy-duty boots so I have lent him my old pair of freshly-resoled Zamberlans. They are not working out. Behind me I hear a hair-raising shriek which chills my bones. I turn to see him doing a sloppy pirouette against the sky. Then he lunges for the rock and clings for dear life with both arms to a coffin of sandstone. I'm thinking that this prophet of doom may be right. "It's the shoes," he says. The new waffle tread, he claims, sticks to the rock. I don't know what he's talking about. "It's like walking across glass with suction cups," he insists. I think he's crazy but we swap shoes. Surprisingly, this seems to help.

Below the worst of the boulder jam soars a towering pillar of Moenkopi sandstone. Leaning against the base of this pillar was once a rock adorned with carvings and paintings of chickens, the Chicken Shrine. I see no pictures on any of the stones here now, but when Don Talayesva hiked the Salt Trail in 1912, he and his companions left offerings of dough and feathers here and crowed a little in order to assure success with poultry. The other places chronicled in Talayesva's account are perhaps impossible to recognize because the descriptions of them are vague. The Chicken Shrine, however, was undoubtedly at the foot of this unmistakable spire. Along the way, I have looked for rock art or pottery, but there is nothing. A hiker has told me that he once discovered, a little off the route, a large portion of an Anasazi pot decorated with a jagged black and white design. He also described to me a place where straightened sticks, looking a little like arrow shafts, were concealed in a small cave. I find the spot and take some pictures. Just what these sticks mean or how old they are is a mystery, though they appear as if they are some kind of an offering. In another small alcove lower in the formation, I find another dowel-like stick.

Another hiker has also told me that atop the Redwall above the river lie two large cairns of jasper. A Hopi friend told him that these were built by Hopi pilgrims over the centuries. At the end of a Salt Expedition each devotee would, it was said, leave a single stone. If this story is true, it might well provide a documentary record of the expeditions from ages past. An archeologist could count the stones and arrive at the number of devotees who had made the journey. It would be reasonable to assume, of course, that the tradition of placing a rock did not necessarily start with the first or even the hundredth pilgrimage, but it would tell how many had worshipped at the Salt Mines or the Sipapu since the tradition started. Another Native American friend, however, said that these cairns looked like graves. The story behind these rock piles may never be known. Looking to *Sun Chief* does not help to resolve the question; Don Talayesva mentions nothing of these cairns in the record of his Salt Expedition.

Tom and I descend farther into the canyon following cairns. It's easy to stay on course and the canyon relents a little from time to time; we sometimes find ourselves striding along on an obvious trail. On the left-hand side of the canyon, for instance, a long, flat stone "walkway" traverses an overhang along a wall. Nearby, in a sandy little basin above a huge, dry plunge-pool, we drop our packs. Getting dark. We have passed small tinajas full of water, each of them reminding me of the weighty load I'm bearing on my back. I haven't drunk one drop. We spread out our flimsy pads and drape our heavy Hollofil bags on top.

Winter is a quiet time in the canyon. We have seen no lizards, no squirrels, not even insects, aside from a few pallid winged grasshoppers. Tom's total bird count: one rock wren. We boil water on my tiny Honeybird gas stove and pour cups of boiling water into pouches of freeze-dried backpacker stroganoff and lasagna. I've left my wood burning stove at home. Though it is convenient on a long trek, on a short one it is not worth the hassle of keeping the thing stoked and putting up with soot begrimed pots.

I prepare dinner with such care that I wonder a little if cooking is not the entire object of the hike. Into the lasagna I dump the entire contents of a small container of parmesan cheese which I stir in with chopsticks. I also add a square of real longhorn cheddar, a handful of dried mushrooms and a spoonful of dehydrated onions. I've got something else also. Wonderful Mexican Cotija cheese, salty and rich. I crumble a chunk over the top. To make it even better I include a special ingredient—chile pequin. This is in the form of an orange powder I have prepared by pulverizing the small, dried chiles in a coffee grinder and sifting the result through a wire mesh so that no remnants of the yellow seeds remain. Hotter than the hubs of Hell, a small pinch sprinkled over any dish will add the necessary fire. Every hiker has his own crazy ingredients; dreaming up recipes is half the fun. The light continues fading, and as we finish eating, I feel a sense of satisfaction that we have timed things well enough to avoid the misery of cooking in the dark.

Soon it is night. Satellites fall across the sky and the long white needles of meteors flare like sparks struck from flint. We watch Orion, the Seven Sisters, and just under the canopy of stars, the silent lights of passing planes which I imagine are glittering indecipherable codes, each spelling a single word over and over. We lean back against a stone drinking cold bottled beer. Tom says he sees ghost lights twinkling like fireflies against the black shadow of a cliff and I'll be damned if I don't see them too. After a while the rising moon turns the sky into a mistiness full of light and depth, the cliffs emerge from the shadows, and the mysterious lights disappear.

You don't see such shows of light either real or imagined with a roof over your head. My friends who don't hike often seem appalled when they learn that I rarely pack a tent. They shudder to imagine a night uninsulated by at least a protective film of nylon. But having walked away from the machinery of civilization, I am completely at ease. The closest automobile is the one we left at the rim miles away. But aren't there mountain lions, they ask. Not many, and what good would a tent do? The claws of a lion bent on my demise would slash like straight razors through any fabric. But snakes, they insist. Aren't you afraid of snakes? Not really. Rattlers are uncommon here and I would count seeing one as a benefit. I have yet to see a pink Grand Canyon rattlesnake.

Admittedly, a snake bite here would be nothing but trouble. Tom's doomsaying makes me dwell on this a little. What exactly are the chances of a rattlesnake bite? Aside from their scarcity, the fact that rattlesnakes are not particularly aggressive makes them unlikely assailants. I have read that the profile for a rattlesnake bite victim generally involves the following scenario: male in his twenties, drunk, *holding* snake. Most other bites occur when the dumbbell is trying to harass or kill the rattler. Stumbling upon a rattlesnake or sharing a sleeping bag with one are not common ways of getting bitten.

I recall a snake story which occurred near the ultimate terminus of this very drainage. In his classic account of his 1907 expedition to Sonora's Pinacate Mountains, *Camp-Fires on Desert and Lava*, William Hornaday recounts an anecdote which suggests that even a snake in the hand may not at times be any more dangerous than one in the bush. The story regarded his geographer, Godfrey Sykes, who wished to set his aneroid for a more accurate measurement of the Pinacates' elevation. The only sure way to do this was to walk to sea level, to the sandy shores of the Sea of Cortez, a couple dozen miles to the south. There he could set the pressure-altitude indicator of the device to zero.

Aside from being a good geographer and as respected a writer as Hornaday, Sykes was also one hell of a hiker. One morning, without telling the others, he set out for the sea. Having made the difficult crossing of the sand hills, he found walking across the flats easy. At the gulf, he adjusted the scale of his instrument and after gathering a few shell specimens for Hornaday, he started back. The full moon illuminated the way and he arrived at camp at half past one that morning. His pedometer measured 43 miles. There was, however, an incident on the way back. I best let Mr. Sykes tell the rest of it himself:

"The net zoological result of my pasear was a few little birds of unknown species, a jackrabbit or two, a coyote and a little coiled up rattlesnake evidently suffering from the chilly night air. I put my hand on the snake, thinking it was a shell, and never discovered what kind of snake it was until, as he slid through my fingers, I felt his rattles! At that I bid him a hurried adieu and left him to find warmer quarters."

I know only one person who has suffered a rattlesnake bite. My friend of many years ago, Joe Callahan, was once bitten by a sidewinder. He was trying to force feed a pet rattler by stuffing a mouse down its throat. In the process he inadvertently inserted his thumb into the snake's mouth. Both fangs got him. In this case the bite should not have been a dangerous one because, as a precaution, Joe had milked the sidewinder just before attempting to feed it. Joe squeezed his thumb and two pure red droplets appeared. No venom seemed to have been injected. Thinking he was in the clear, he put the snake back into its cage and went about his business.

A half hour later he noticed a dark red line of discoloration moving slowly up his arm following the course of the radial artery. His wife called the hospital and soon he was greeted by the excited staff of doctors, nurses, candy stripers and janitors who were waiting eagerly at the emergency room door. By now Joe's face was swelling up. I don't remember whether he was given antivenin or not, but the snake nearly killed him.

Joe was always careless with snakes. He was intrigued by them and collected all kinds. One day on the Reservation along I-40 near Sanders, Joe stopped to pick up a hitchhiker, a guy he knew, Emerson Roanhorse, who was hitchhiking along the frontage road. "Ya' 'at eeh, Emerson. Where you headed?" Emerson pointed ahead Navajo-style with a pursing of the lips and an upward nod of the head. "Goin' to my Aunt's, Joe. Right up here by Houck."

"How's your sister doing, Emerson?"

"She's okay. Working at Whiting Brothers."

At this point, Joe braked for a stop sign and a burlap bag slid out from under the front seat. A rattler slithered out. As a general thing, Navajo men are not much shaken by rattlesnakes, but the unexpected appearance of one inside a car is enough to test anyone's resolve. Joe's passenger must have weighed two hundred pounds, but he went through the window like a jackrabbit. The window was rolled half way up and how he got through without breaking the glass is hard to say.

Joe was immediately contrite. "Damn, I'm sorry, Emerson. I didn't know that would happen. Hang on. I'll resack him.

"Ah, Ch'iidii! You dumb bastard. Why don't you tell me you got a snake in there. Are you crazy?"

"Sorry. Sorry."

Emerson cooled down.

"Just put him back in the bag. Hurry up. I'm already missing dinner."

Another time, on holiday, Joe was tubing down the Salt River near Phoenix when he came upon a fine black and yellow kingsnake in the brush along the shore. Enthusiastically, he grabbed it and wrapped it around his neck and began paddling to meet his party of friends at an island in the middle of the stream. Now the kingsnake has a reputation for being an amiable creature, a fair pet as far as snakes go, but this one opened its mouth and grabbed the soft flesh of Joe's throat like the clamp on a jumper cable. At the island Joe paced up and down the shore cradling the snake, followed by his sympathetic companions.

Meanwhile, floating clusters of tubers, many beery and unsteady on their feet, arrived at the island full of pitying interest. A crowd began to gather. Joe and his snake had become a riparian attraction. "Over here!" someone would yell across the water. "A guy's got a snake on him. Hangin' on his throat!"

"No shit?" Then, "Damn! I'm stuck in an eddy. Don't let him get away. I'll be right there." (The sound of furious paddling.)

Joe was thinking that he could do without a portion of this attention. His main concern was how to dislodge the snake without injuring it. Every one of the hundred and ten spectators, though, had the same idea. "Burn him off!" they cried. "Here!" and they each thrust a flaming Bic lighter in Joe's face.

Even with the snake hanging painfully from his neck, Joe couldn't help but marvel at the excitability of these wet, slightly-toasted individuals. Almost all of them had lighters which they adjusted so that a foot of orange flame gushed out. Inspired by many twelve packs, they were fired with an earnest desire to serve him, a boozy sympathy, a philanthropic zeal almost. But at this point all Joe wanted was for them to go away. "Jump in the water," one suggested. "Drown the sonofabitch off."

That seemed like a fair idea. Joe jumped in.

In the annals of human arrogance there is scarcely an example which equals Joe Callahan's attempt to hold his breath longer than a kingsnake. In short, he couldn't do it, and these two marvels of nature remained connected until the reptile tired of the game and dropped off of its own accord.

In the morning Tom and I leave our packs at our camp in the wash and trek down to a deep fissure with huge impassable pour-offs. The route crosses the wash above and ascends in the form of a faint trail to the top of the Redwall where it continues a long pace before dropping down to the river. We trudge up the steep slope. Below we see the shining water. The bluest river in the world? I have no doubt, though as I have mentioned, it has another face when it runs a walnut brown and at the confluence it mixes with the green water of the Big Colorado the way cream swirls into coffee.

We've been here long enough. I've promised my young son that I'll stay closer to home. He worries that I'll never come back. He shouldn't. The eight days I spent in the Gorge with my brother Jeff were the longest time I'd ever spent away from him, and I wonder a little that it has already been two years since Jeff and I walked along the sands of the turquoise waters below Salt Trail Canyon. Just what dreams compelled us to hike the Gorge are already fading into memory.

Many wilderness travelers express their desire to find a spiritual enlightenment in nature, an answer to the mystery of their lives. I am all for this, but personally have long since given up such seeking for, to me, the answers seem only to appear in the form of the most arcane metaphors, at best disquieting and always indecipherable. I count myself fortunate to have been so untroubled by spiritual longing for I suspect that this is because I have found enough to satisfy me. An experience itself unencumbered by a recondite quest is more than sufficient.

I remember a Navajo woman I once bought jewelry from asking, "Why do you do that? Why do you go down in there?"

"For fun," I told her, and it was a true answer.

The river is just as I have remembered it, a milky blue. We have no time to linger here. We have jobs and obligations. Against my inclinations, I try to sense something of myself in the huge and timeless canyon and find nothing. Time flies more quickly for a man than it does for a canyon and a canyon has no promises to keep. We ascend to a high place overlooking the shining blue river and listen to the white sound of rushing water.

16
Little Colorado Day Six
Camp Beamer Late Afternoon

As Jeff and I continue downstream from the Sipapu, we find trails along the shore, trails with footprints. River runners sometimes hike up this far and it is wonderful to dispense with the route-finding and mindlessly follow the paths, however vague, through the tammies and cattails. A few miles down we see people. Aside from the talking specks on the rim at mile ten, they are the first people we've seen in six days. A group of river runners basks on a rock shelf above the blue water. The brilliant colors of their swimsuits glare unnaturally against the subtle hues of the Gorge. From here we continue on another mile or two, at last reaching the Colorado where clusters of boats are tied and river guides lead orderly lines of clients looking a little like kindergarten classes, each passenger still wearing a life jacket, along a wide shelf on the other side of the Little C.

Just upstream is the Walter Powell Route. Not in any way a trail, the route is merely a passage, a way out of the canyon which, it is said, John Wesley Powell's brother explored during the Powell expedition of 1869. Once in a blue moon, a canyoneer enamored of history, or just for the fun of it, will climb the Walter Powell to the rim.

Jeff and I rest the balance of the day in the shade of the cliffs along the left bank of the blue Little C watched by curious spiny lizards. Time to crack open the two cans of tuna we've been saving. We kill off our remainder of Triscuits crackers by smashing them up and mixing them in our cups with the tuna. I add a mashed up package of peanut butter and cheese sandwich crackers. It tastes great chased with ice-cold grape Kool Aid made from the Big C's chilly water. The sun here is ferocious. My thermometer registers 125 degrees. It must be broken. But maybe not. In any case, it couldn't be much more than ten degrees off. Hiking out along the Beamer Trail in this kind of heat would be the worst kind of folly.

I swim across the blue, opaque water to where river runners are disembarking and ask around about the Beamer Trail. I find the trip leader and tell him we've come from Cameron and want to find the Beamer. He looks a little clean-cut for a boatman, at least for the ones I remember when I ran the river a little in the seventies. He has clean clothes and a real haircut.

"Cameron? What is that, forty miles?"

"More like sixty," I brag.

"That's a helluva hike. What's it like in there?"

"Fine."

"How's the trail?"

"Oh, there isn't any trail."

"Any rattlesnakes?"

"Naw...Gophersnake as big as a fire hose."

The young guide knows nothing about the Beamer except that he has seen people up there. "I think it begins just up there over the Tapeats formation. You've got a full moon tonight," he added. "You might walk it in the night." He looked at me earnestly. "No shit. Beat the heat."

He tells me that Palisades Creek is only three miles downstream. But he is talking river miles. By our route, the distance will be twice that. The sun sets behind the cliffs. We say good-bye to the spiny lizards and climb up through the fading light to the foot of the Beamer. Not too hot at all with the sun blown out, but the trail is tiring, winding down into and up out of drainages again and again. The worst part though is the cliffs. There is rumored to be an upper branch of the Beamer, safer than the cliff-hugging lower path. But we are not on it. Confirmed acrophobes, we are mortified to see that the trail contours ledges with drop-offs hundreds of feet deep buffered only by two-foot slopes of loose, slippery shale. In places the track is less than one foot wide along a ragged cliff against which our packs sometimes scrape. Any careless stumble, any false step could result in a decidedly spectacular, one-hundred-percent-fatal plunge. The river guide's suggestion to walk at night is crazy.

We do have one lucky circumstance. The wind is not blowing. It is said that in this part of the canyon driving afternoon winds are formidable enough to grab an external frame pack and wrench a hiker off the edge. We creep along swearing softly and uttering little incantations to comfort us.

Before the light dims completely, we shed the packs in one of the rocky washes away from the edge and get ready to cook. Soon we are boiling noodles and draining the excess liquid into our cups for coffee. No water up here at Camp Beamer. Got to conserve it. Pad Tai noodles are on the menu for dinner tonight. I bought them at Lee Lee's, a lavish Oriental supermarket in Chandler, Arizona, a backpacker's gold mine for lightweight pasta. The package contains clear rice noodles and two packets of sauce along with a midget envelope of red hot chile powder, perfect backpacker food—fast cooking, and packing a walloping 1000 calories. They are also delicious, fiery hot. But tonight they are not enough. Into the noodles I mix half an envelope of leftover mashed potatoes for good measure. We lie on our sleeping bags as the sky darkens around a white, silent moon. Somewhere very nearby, are the sacred Hopi salt mines, the second War Twin, and the fantastic medicine bowl stalagmite we will never see.

But there is something else on our minds. We have looked across the river to Chuar and Temple buttes and like many who pass them via the trail or the river, we think of something sad and horrific that happened here years ago. The years have passed and few people remember much of the tragedy. There are as many versions of the event as there are lives touched by it and it's difficult to know just how to tell the story. I found one account though, that might as well as any other, offer a vantage from which to tell of it. After our hike, I spoke to Ted Page of Massachusetts about an article he had written for *Boston Magazine* called "The Accidental Guardian." Though the tragedy happened years before he was born, it had for him the most profound significance.

17

Out of the Sky

It was August 6th 1999, Hiroshima Day, and three men were hiking New Hampshire's Mount Washington, a yearly family tradition. It is unusual for non-Japanese Americans to honor the memories of Hiroshima's victims, but the day held significance for the older hiker, William Page. It was here on New England's highest mountain that he had chosen to remember each year the Pacific War where he had served at sea and on Okinawa, and to impart to his sons perhaps a little of what the experience had meant. His sons stood and listened as the old man began his almost formal annual speech. Below them the Lake of the Clouds appeared and disappeared in a swiftly drifting summer mist. Perhaps he had much to celebrate this Hiroshima Day, for had the bomb not been dropped, he would almost certainly have died in the invasion of Japan. But he did not feel that way. Nothing, he told his sons, could justify such cruelty. Though the bomb had saved his life, his sons sensed that if he could have chosen he would not have had it so. Even though John and Ted Page had heard their father's story many times, they still found it moving. But this year he was to include an addendum to the narrative that would stun them. William Page was 77 years old now and maybe not likely to make the speech on Mt. Washington again. This summer for the first time, they had taken the cog railway to the summit in order to avoid the strenuous uphill portion. "There's one last thing I need to tell you," he began. "Something happened a long time ago."

The story was a simple one, perhaps even a little trite like those sentimental, apocryphal stories religious people tell about miracles but, according to his son, William Page did not ascribe a moral to it as if it were a parable with a simple, clarifying explication.

It was the morning of June 30, 1956 and World War II was long gone. William Page waited for a flight at Los Angeles Airport. Like most Americans of the Greatest Generation, the horrors, the privation and the lost summers were behind him, the experience having left him curiously grounded. The war had brought into sharp focus the value of job, house and family. Ted Page imagined his father then as looking a little like Gregory Peck, with a charcoal gray suit, dark hair and glasses, and as exuding a quiet composure visible even at this young age. You could pick him out of a crowd. Anyone relying on the kindness of strangers could see him.

So it was that June morning. "Excuse me. I was wondering if you could do me a favor," a woman asked him. "I understand you have a ticket for the earlier flight. Would you mind switching with me?" She was in a great hurry to reach Chicago, she explained. He could take the later flight. William Page looked at the attractive, neatly dressed middle aged woman. Why not? He was in no big hurry. "Sure," he said. The two swapped tickets and the grateful stranger boarded United Airlines Flight 718, a Douglas DC 7 which departed at 9:04 AM off runway 25 L. Three minutes earlier, a fully loaded Lockheed Super Constellation named the Star of the Seine, had left the same airport bound for Kansas City. Both planes would be crossing the Painted Desert. William Page waited at the terminal until the later flight was ready. Then he boarded the plane, found the woman's seat and sat down in it.

The plane William Page did not take was piloted by Captain Robert F. Shirley and First Officer Robert W. Harms. Out the window the two pilots no doubt observed the departure of what they would have called a Superconnie, a graceful craft with three distinctive paddle-like vertical stabilizers on the tail. After takeoff United's DC 7 was vectored through the same overcast as the Super Constellation, TWA Flight 2. United 718 headed east as it ascended toward its proposed cruising altitude of 21,000 feet where the DC 7 would continue past check points at Needles, Painted Desert, Durango, Pueblo, and on until it reached Chicago. The captain reported his position over Riverside and then over Palm Springs, indicated that the plane was still climbing to 21,000 feet, and estimated a time of arrival at the Needles checkpoint at 10 o'clock and the Painted Desert at 10:34. The flight continued on at 280 knots. The CAA communications station at Needles received the flight's position report at 9:58. Here the captain stated that the plane had reached its 21,000 foot cruising altitude and adjusted the estimated time of arrival at the

Painted Desert to 10:31.

Meanwhile, TWA Flight 2, piloted by Captain Jack Gandy and copilot James Ritner, was reporting over California's Lake Mojave. Their flight plan proposed a cruising altitude of 19,000 feet and an airspeed of 270 knots but at 9:21 Gandy requested a change to 21,000 feet. He was refused approval because of traffic (Flight 718). He then requested a change to 1000 on top, meaning he would ascend to one thousand feet above the clouds, and was cleared. At 9:59 Flight 2 reported its altitude and estimated arrival time at the 321-degree radial of the Winslow OMNI radar range station (Painted Desert). The Star of the Seine was still 1000 feet on top of the thunderclouds which soared this day to 20,000 feet, and would cross the Painted Desert line of position at 10:31.

Neither plane reported in over the Painted Desert. When regular ground communications could not raise them, a radio search utilizing numerous radio frequencies receivable by the planes was carried out. Neither plane responded. The minutes piled up. Nothing. The flight controllers investigating the situation realized early on the most obvious explanation for the silence, but they persisted, perhaps unwilling to accept what they feared was true. The Painted Desert check-in was an hour and twenty minutes overdue. At 11:51 a missing aircraft alert was broadcast and search and rescue procedures implemented.

While the flights had been routed through the same line of position at the same time, this in itself did not pose any great concern. The Painted Desert line of position was just that—a line—not a point of convergence, and this linear position stretched almost 175 miles. The planes were only to pass the same line eastbound at the same time. Even with the matching altitudes of 21,000 feet, it was a million to one shot that they had collided. But if not a collision, then what? That both had crashed independently in unrelated incidents seemed even less likely. The altitudes and times spoke volumes. The flight controllers had to face facts. The impossible had happened. The planes had run into each other. It just couldn't be anything else.

Every passing minute of silence seemed to confirm the awful conclusion, and then the minutes became hours. No transmission had been received from the missing planes since United reported over Needles at 9:58 and TWA just past Lake Mojave at 9:55—at least any intelligible communication. There had been recorded, however, an unidentified radio signal that neither the aeronautical operators at Salt Lake City, nor those in San Francisco could at the time understand. It was received and tape-recorded at 10:31.

At dinner that evening two brothers, Palen and Henry Hudgin, operators of Grand Canyon Airlines, a scenic flight service operating over Grand Canyon National Park, heard of the missing planes. Earlier that Saturday they had noted smoke in the Canyon near the Colorado River at its confluence with the Little C, but had dismissed it as a lightning strike. Now they sped to the scene in a light plane, able to make only one pass before darkness closed in. One pass was enough. Below them, smashed against a 700-foot cliff of the

6500-foot Chuar Butte, lay the melted, smoldering wreckage of an airliner spilling over another 700-foot cliff like black tar. Some of it was still afire. The plane was shattered into a million pieces. The Hudgin brothers, however, viewed the wreck through the experienced eyes of men who knew planes, and recognized one fragment as part of the triple tail of a constellation. Nearby lay the shattered remains of another plane. "Everything is wreckage," they reported. "There are certainly no survivors."

On Sunday the scraps of the Superconnie were identified. The pieces were somewhat bigger than those of the other plane and lay one half mile south on the northern cliffs of Temple Butte. Had the airliners fallen just a half mile in practically any direction, they would have come down on a vast plateau where the recovery of bodies and the investigation of the wrecks would have been relatively simple. Helicopters could with ease, ferry in crews for the terrible work. There were even dirt roads meandering atop the plateau. But the location of the wreckage posed many dangers for investigators. The reports from rangers were filled with depressing superlatives about the hazards. Assistant Park Superintendent Charles Shevlin told reporters that "the crash scene was in one of the most inaccessible places on the North American continent." He added that it would take at least five days to reach the wrecks on foot and doubted that even helicopters could get to them. This was not hyperbole. The section of the Canyon where the planes fell was one thousand feet above the river and the formations of rock to which much of the wreckage and many of the bodies clung, could only be described as vertical. The planes also had fallen on the more remote and isolated north side of the Canyon. Complicating the recovery efforts further was the wind factor. The first crews dropped off were stranded overnight because the wind was too great for helicopters to fly in. Short on sleeping bags, several men took shelter from the dry storm that night by sleeping in the rubber body bags brought in for the corpses.

It was apparent right away that excavating the remains and recovering all the bodies would be difficult, if not impossible, and there was much discussion of just how it might be done. The Hudgin brothers recognized from the beginning that only helicopters could access the area with any kind of efficiency, and that even these could not safely operate alongside the plunging cliffs. The terrain was so steep and dangerous that to disgorge recovery teams from helicopters meant putting them at extreme risk. Only the most experienced climbers had any business on the steeper parts of the buttes where much of the wreckage lay.

The fire caused by the disaster was enough to melt aircraft engines and what was left of the bodies was, for the most part, unrecognizable. The problem remained how to reach them all. It would take world class climbers to do it. Swiss mountaineers from Zurich were flown in for the grisly job of sacking the remains of the victims in the fierce summer heat of the canyon. But the Grand Canyon was a far cry from the Alps, requiring specialized skills which hardly existed at the time. Even these experts were not wholly prepared for the unique challenges. They arrived wearing their traditional woolen knickers and long sleeved, checkered shirts.

From the river the immensity of the canyon cannot be fully perceived, and even from the rim one does not experience the total effect of the panorama. Descending into the canyon, however, the whole giant scene opens as if one has been swallowed from both above and below. Temple and Chuar buttes become only two of many impressive forms fading into the distance. The Swiss climbers might have forgotten for a moment their miserable task and marveled a little at the soaring red limestone cliffs, the shale and mudstone hills softening the warmer colors with shades of blue and lavender, and the patterns of cloud shadows. The river the Swiss climbers were to look down upon from Temple Butte was unlike anything in Europe. TWA's Star of the Seine did not lie above a peaceful green meander like the airliner's namesake. The Colorado was a Spartan river, as yet undammed, muddy and rock-edged with frothing sections of white, its banks bordered only thinly by tamarisk and willow struggling to live among the rocks.

It was a ghastly job. One of the first to arrive on the scene was Air Force doctor Donald Hunter, who upon his return, expressed his hope that he would never live to see such a thing again. "The most of any person I saw was half a woman."

William Page's sons were not the only beneficiaries of a dicey fortune. Luck also smiled on another family that fateful June morning. Thomas Magness, his wife Jeanette, thirteen-year-old daughter, Dinah Sue, and three-year-old son, Thomas Junior, had boarded a TWA plane to find that the flight attendants had miscounted. They were short one seat. Magness, an employee of Bonanza Airlines out of Phoenix and transporting his family as non-revenue passengers, was given the choice between remaining aboard with Thomas Jr. sitting on someone's lap, or catching the next available plane, TWA Flight 2. They stayed on board.

William Page did not ascribe to the incident any supernatural interventions. He was a Unitarian, a denomination which values reason and freedom of belief, and whose members sometimes refer to themselves jokingly as atheists with children. He did not believe that God had stepped in and saved him for some arcane purpose like building a church. A rationalist, he believed that "the world was fascinating enough without concocting fairy tales." But he did bring away the conviction that he was the beneficiary of some kind of grace and resolved to make count a life which had been unwittingly purchased for a small kindness.

The work in the canyon was eventually finished. The recovery of bodies did, after all, bring back some remains that were identifiable, nine of the 70 aboard Flight 2 and 29 of the 58 aboard Flight 718. The rest were sealed in coffins and interred in common plots at Flagstaff's Citizens Cemetery and Grand Canyon Village Cemetery. As for the cause of the crash, the conclusion was simple. After all, some of the first metal fragments retrieved clearly revealed that the planes had swapped paint. The final probable cause of the accident was that "the pilots did not see each other in time to avoid the collision." Indeed, it was entirely conceivable that the pilots did not see each other at all. Detailed reconstruction of the events revealed that the left aileron tip of the DC 7 first struck the fuselage of the Super Constellation tearing it open from the tail all the way to the main cabin door. The Superconnie's tail fell off immediately. Most of the DC 7's left wing was sheared away in the collision causing that plane to spin down completely out of control.

The unidentified radio signal received by controllers in San Francisco and Salt Lake City came from the DC 7 as the panicked pilots struggled to make the falling plane fly again. The recording of the transmission was studied carefully in hopes that it would shed some light on the specifics of the accident. Perhaps the events leading up to the crash could be ascertained. The recording was examined utilizing spectrographic analysis, binaural listening and "speech stretching" techniques. These uncovered the context of a brief message: "Salt Lake, area (or ah), seven eighteen...we are going in." During the brief interruption of the sentence indicated by the ellipsis, another speaker could be heard yelling what was probably, "Pull up!" The principal speaker, later determined to be First Officer Harms, spoke between 100 and 200 decibels above the normal male voice spectrograms. The other voice was well above that of a female's voice, though it was assumed to be that of Captain Shirley or Flight Engineer Girardo Fiore. Though it begged no explanation, the CAA report on the crash dutifully concluded that the pitch of the voices and other factors of the analysis indicated that the pilots were under extreme distress.

Although investigators interviewed several witness who thought that they might have seen the collision, only one person was located who they believed might have actually observed it. He was a motorist near Winslow traveling on Route 66 almost 80 miles away. All he saw was a puff of smoke high in the distant sky and what appeared to be two objects falling into the clouds.

Neither pilot was operating his aircraft in any way out of the ordinary. Neither was out of compliance with any flight rules or procedures. Since they were each flying "off the control band," that is, beyond the responsibility of ground controllers, they were essentially "on their own." It was their responsibility to maintain a safe distance between themselves and other planes in uncontrolled air space. Unfortunately, in the three dimensions of flight, this is often exceedingly difficult to do. There are cockpit limitations on vision, intervening clouds and distracting flight duties of both officers. In addition to this, there are factors of time and speed to consider, coupled with the limitations of human vision. By the time an approaching plane is sighted, it may already be too late to avoid it. The possibility that the pilots were maneuvering the planes to give the passengers a view of the Canyon was noted by the Civil Aeronautics Board's report, but there was no way to determine whether this was a factor in the collision.

The report on the accident also explained that while

TWA Flight 2 was advised of traffic at 21,000 feet, no advisory of TWA's altitude was given to Flight 718. Still, everyone was operating by the book. Obviously the book needed to be rewritten. The consequences of the accident were profound. The operations and procedures for guiding air traffic in the United States were forever changed, the CAA was eventually dismantled and a new agency, the FAA, put in place.

For years the wreckage of the disaster lay exposed high on the rocky cliffs of Chuar and Temple buttes. Just downstream from the confluence the passengers of the increasingly popular river trips would turn and look up at the glinting silver pieces of aluminum. It was a somber sight. The mood of every river trip changed here as if the boat had passed under a cloud shadow, and the people were quiet for a while. Boatmen often turned the rafts around and floated backwards so the passengers could more easily observe the gleaming metal high above.

The passage of time and the extraction of the visible scraps of aluminum from the cliffs have had their effect. The section of the park whose beauty was once tinged by sorrowful thoughts can be looked at with new eyes. There is little left glittering on the sunlit bluffs. Only the area's remoteness, which so vexed the rescuers and investigators in 1956, remains. River parties still stop at the confluence for lunch, and a swim in the warm, turquoise waters of the Little Colorado. Afterwards, they continue downstream past Chuar and Temple buttes never looking back.

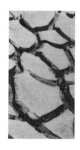

18

Little Colorado
Day Seven Camp Tanner

I awake before dawn as usual and watch the night. Jeff is still sleeping. Camp Beamer is harsher than the sandy beaches we have slept on the last five nights. The floor of the wash is solid stone and we have lain between sharp, broken and jumbled boulders, quite unlike the more ordered, rounded stones of the Gorge. Still, the soft, familiar peacefulness of a canyon morning is here. Silent bats flutter in the twilight sky. Jeff gets up and we crouch over the stove as our coffee boils. We are a little short on water, but we are confident that we'll make it to the river all right. We begin while the sky is still gray and the air still cool.

As we march along the narrow path, we look down on the broad, black backs of roosting ravens who survey the river from ledges on the cliffs. It is an odd perspective. From above, the ravens seem somehow surreal. They crouch on the craggy rocks where the rising breeze sometimes raises a cowlick of black feathers. I am reminded of those malevolent flying monkeys in *The Wizard of Oz*. From our high place we can also see two dark forms swimming lazily in the green shallows of the river far below. My midget binoculars are fogged up with moisture, completely useless. Without them I cannot tell if I am looking at beavers or otters.

From the Beamer Trail I can see the vastness of the distance we must cover, and measure the grandness of the canyon as its shadows unfold with the rising sun. "Look where we have to go. All the way up there, around that turn to God knows where and then along the edge again."

Jeff looks where I'm pointing. "It'll drop down into Palisades Creek somewhere over there. I hope." The distance seems so far that we are almost disheartened, but we know that we will, like determined mites, cover the whole extent step by tiny step. More sheer drop-offs test our resolve but soon enough we reach a rocky section of trail which winds down to Palisades Creek. At the bottom we find the square outlines of a stone ruin. The sight of the ruin gives me a jolt. We have missed Beamer's Cabin! Miles behind us, just a pace upstream of the rivers' junction on the left bank of the little C, lay the historical cabin built by miner Ben Beamer, the trail's namesake. In 1869 John Wesley Powell described only an old Indian ruin at the location. It was this ruin that Ben Beamer was later to refurbish, rearranging the stone blocks and adding a window and door. Here the hermitic prospector lived during the late 1800s. We must have walked right past it. Oh, well. You can't do everything right. We fill our bottles with icy river water and rest in cool, leafy shadows by the shore.

The sun rises like a sword over Furnace Flats as we begin a brain-roasting walk along a well-traveled trail which has been edged for great distances with stones, giving the area a state park effect. This labor was no doubt done by winter visitors. It's much too hot to disassemble any portion of it. We take a break in the sparse shade near the river. Then we brave the heat again, making Tanner at noon but not before climbing up one last stretch of the Dox Formation and traversing another drop-off. This one falls fifty feet into the river. A backpacker lounges at a shady camp near the shore. He is a park volunteer on vacation from his job on the rim at the Tusayan Museum. He will be the only person we will see between the confluence and the head of Tanner.

At the foot of the trail near the river, we rest under a shady copse of tammies. It is a comfortable spot to hole-up and wait out the sun. There is also a small cave here. Anyone who has hiked Tanner knows the place. We cook up stroganoff and dried mushrooms in the shadows. Almost at the end of the trek, we now notice how light our packs have become. I have only two bags of macaroni and cheese, some crackers, a pouch of hot chocolate, five tea bags and ten pieces of hard candy left. Some physical changes also become apparent. I've shed ten pounds off my 185 pound frame and Jeff, who started out weighing just 130, has lost perhaps five.

Our friends the spiny lizards visit us. Jeff catches a fly, crimps its wings, and tosses it onto the dusty ground. It buzzes furiously, trying to get some purchase on the air, but a lizard hears and snaps him up. The lizards have become our favorite animals on the trip, having visited us at every camp. They are active, involved little reptiles and seem very tame.

Sometimes they appear angry, doing threatening pushups, and sometimes only curious, coming very close and cocking their heads, just looking. The males have bright blue patches and their rough, "spiny" scales are often spangled with yellow or dusty red. Their bulbous eyes seem to swivel independently, giving them a chameleon-like appearance. I am thinking that they would make good pets, but I am to find that they have a tendency to bite when handled.

Like the Palisades, Tanner Canyon is wide and open. The sun takes its time before finding a cliff to hide behind. By now it's late, but we are ready to start the climb out. During our respite, I have been prehydrating, sipping river water in the shadowy grotto of tamarisks until I have drunk well over a gallon. We slog up the wash and ascend the hills on and on in the hot shade until it is too dark to walk. A mile from the foot of the Redwall and I'm still not thirsty. We find a wide, flat place at the top of a rise and dump the packs. Camp Tanner is cool and slightly breezy, and we have the sensation of camping above things now. We lie in our sleeping bags at the edge of the trail and fall like stones into our last dark night in the canyon.

High on the eastern side of the canyon lies one of the most sublime viewpoints from the rim, Cape Solitude. One summer in a moment of caprice, I attempted an overnighter from Desert View Watchtower across the Palisades of the Desert to the Cape. I passed Comanche Point, another fine overlook, and continued along a disused jeep trail that wound through rocky little canyons and up hills and over brushy flats. The Grand Canyon yawned open on my left, but I seldom saw it. To the right lay graceful Cedar Mountain and then Gold Hill, and beyond them, to the east, lay the Gorge cut starkly into a vast plateau receding into the distance. From such vantages one can understand why hiker John Annerino described the Gorge as *"Brobdingnagian* in proportions," an allusion to Swift's imaginary land of giants in *Gulliver's Travels*. To anyone but the superjock hiker, a trip to Cape Solitude is a two-night affair. Short on water, I turned back, but not before finding the outlines of ancient corrals and the ruins of a stone block house with an artfully crafted little chiminea built into the masonry of a corner. Somewhere also on the plateau lies the tire of an airliner sinking into the soil.

And here I experienced a curious and powerful feeling of déjà vu. I had been here before. Not at the confluence on foot or by raft, but here high above looking down. It was a feeling somehow linked with the beauty and tragedy of the place. It was a while before I knew where the feeling had come from; the vision of the aircraft tire half-buried in the plateau had called it up. The awful images of fire and falling were not just yellowing words and photos scanned from brittle microfiche; they were memories both personal and indelible.

It was of a summer afternoon in 1979 when we had made the hop from Phoenix to Flagstaff in a Cessna 172, re-fueling at Flagstaff airport. My friend Barry Ross was at the controls as we headed for the Canyon where we made a few swoops high above the rim over Phantom Ranch where the green ribbon of river slipped under the suspension bridge. Ignoring the map, we moved upstream toward the confluence and soon enough we were peering out the plastic windows to the clear, blue Little C, glittering in the sunshine. We did not think to look for the aircraft debris on Chuar and Temple Buttes, but turned and proceeded directly downstream, again past Desert View Watchtower, Grand Canyon Village and beyond, to the empty wilderness of Great Thumb Mesa and then to Havasu Canyon where we circled the waterfalls of Havasu and Mooney Falls, white threads reaching into tiny blue puddles far below. We could not have known, but another tragedy was drawing nigh. Not long after, Barry would die in his own fiery crash against a rain-swept peak in the Hualapai Mountains.

19
Little Colorado Day Eight
Out

As I lie in the almost light of morning, my mind takes up more tranquil thoughts and wanders downstream to the gulf, the Sea of Cortez, once and still in places yet, untouched, and I see this watercourse as a whole piece, a continuous length of string with a beginning and an end. Far behind us the Little C's water begins its journey to the sea as a clear trout stream in the White Mountains where it meanders from its source, Mt. Baldy, through pine forests and verdant glades. I have backpacked and fished a little along this more smiling aspect of the river. To a desert lover, though, the river only begins to get inspiring when it hits the Painted Desert where its water, when it has any, becomes laden with silt as it rushes, fed by its own red tributaries, across the Navajo reservation. The Rio Puerco which parallels old Route 66 from New Mexico is the major of these.

The Little C has been trekked in its entirety by only one person. In the spring of 1982, former Park Service ranger Nick Berenzenko followed the water from the snowy top of Mt. Baldy, down to and across the Painted Desert and through the muddy Gorge to the confluence—315 miles. It took him 36 days. The most famous landmark along the course is Grand Falls. In the wet season the Little C drops as a brown thundering curtain over wide, limestone shelves before continuing on through a deep canyon. Car access to the falls is by way of a long, sometimes tortuous dirt road, some forty miles northeast of Flagstaff.

Grand Falls was created ages ago by a lava flow spilling from Merriam Crater, next to Sunset Crater, perhaps the most famous of the many cinder cones dotting the landscape. Grand Falls is no small desert cataract. The plunging torrent here rivals Niagara Falls in size and majesty and when the river's running it's an impressive sight. There is an easy trail to the bottom of this canyon and if the river is dry, which is usually, you can climb up on the shelves to explore, or walk downstream where there are petroglyphs on the canyon walls. Years ago my brother Tom and I witnessed a flash flood here. One minute the canyon was bone dry and then, without warning, a wide curtain of Nestle's Quick slipped silently over the edge, then roared. Anyone exploring up there would have been washed over the cliffs.

Under Grand Falls' wide pour-off, one will encounter deep potholes. How these were created is a fascinating process. It might be best to look at how they are formed as a single instance: A chunk of basalt or a big agate of petrified wood, is carried over the edge of the falls and comes to rest on the softer limestone shelf. Rushing water spins the stone. The result is a vague, carved impression, a little bowl if you wish, in the limestone. A bigger flood may wash away the rock but others are coming and they find the shallow depression and also begin to spin and dig. Soon (in geologic terms, this is a process that occurs rather rapidly) there is a genuine hole drilled in the shelf. At the bottom of this now lies a jumble of hard stones and pebbles which the thrashing water agitates, boring a deep, narrow tunnel straight down. Evaporation and the porous nature of the limestone often leave these pot-holes dry. Sometimes such a hole is very narrow and very deep indeed. If you slipped into one, it would be impossible to get out on your own. These "tinajas" are of many shapes and depths. In the winter when they are full, ice forms over the tops. One February I brought my small son to Grand Falls and he spent a happy hour smashing with stones these icy green windows as if they were car windshields.

Along the downstream canyon you can find fossil cephalopods weathering out from the ceilings of high, dry caverns and overhangs. Once on a cold winter day, a friend and I walked down from the falls following a mountain lion's tracks in the snow until they disappeared into a small, square, stone cave up a side canyon. The river continues down past the ruins of Wupatki and on through the Res to Cameron before descending into the Gorge and beyond.

At sunrise, Jeff and I beat the Redwall and walk the long curving trail around Cardenas and Escalante buttes past junipers and buffaloberry, and banana yuccas with their fat, green, pickle-shaped fruit, and arrive at the Stegosaur rock formation before the sun appears. I discard all my water except the side pocket bottle before we begin our last ascent.

It is a hard, long climb out and if I have a tendency to despair, I remember something that Colin Fletcher proposed in his backpackers' bible, *The Complete Walker*, a cardinal rule of travel he called *The Law of Inverse Appreciation*. Says Fletcher:

> "The less there is between you and the environment, the more you appreciate the environment. Every walker knows, even if he has not thought about it, the law's most obvious application: the bigger and more efficient your means of travel, the further you become divorced from the reality through which you are traveling. A man learns a thousand times more about the sea from the Kon Tiki than from the Queen Mary."

I am also reminded of Robert M. Pirsig's *Zen and the Art of Motorcycle Maintenance*. I'd read it years ago and though I thought Pirsig strayed off the subject of motorcycles more often than was fair, he also noted this inverse appreciation idea:

> "...through that car window everything you see is just more TV...On a cycle the frame is gone...that concrete whizzing by five inches below your foot is the real thing, the same stuff you walk on...never removed from immediate consciousness."

Fletcher added an extending corollary to his law: "The further you move away from any impediment of appreciation, the better it is."

The law and its corollary are hard to love as one slogs up the Tanner, back aching, feet hurting, blisters smarting with sweat, taste buds strangely, inexplicably grieving for the lack of a Blueberry Newton, but after an hour on the rim, resting in the shade, the law holds true.

My prehydration and twilight walking have worked better than I could have imagined. I realize that I am going to make it out of Tanner in summer having drunk little more than half a gallon of water. It's a long climb, two hours, before we find ourselves at the end of the switchbacks and walking a gentle rise through the trees where Impressionistic junipers cast blue shadows where they have spilled their berries.

As we approach the trailhead, we cannot help but feel a sense of accomplishment. We have done what not too many have done before. Nearing the rim, it is hard not to rhapsodize over what we have seen. We have explored a pristine, seldom-visited canyon, a canyon of unsurpassed beauty, have walked the Little Colorado River Gorge from beginning to end and come to know it.

Blacktop. The edge of the sloping road to Lipan Point. We pause there, two whiskered, grinning apparitions, wearing clothes the color of mud. A F-350 pickup truck is pulling a trailer as big as an ocean liner. The trailer towers above us bright and clean and new. It takes a long time for the whole thing to pass by.

Bibliography

Abbey, Edward. *Beyond The Wall*. "The Damnation of a Canyon." New York: Holt, Rinehart and Winston, 1971.

--- *Desert Solitaire*. New York: Simon and Schuster, 1968.

Aitchison, Stewart. *A Naturalist's Guide to Hiking the Grand Canyon*. Englewood Cliffs, New Jersey: Prentice Hall, 1985.

Alkire, Robert F. "Fading Rays of Sun Light Crash Debris." *Salt Lake City Tribune*. 2 July, 1956.

Annerino, John. *Hiking the Grand Canyon*. San Francisco: Sierra Club Books, 1993.

Babbitt, Bruce. *Grand Canyon, An Anthology*. Flagstaff, Arizona: Northland Press, 1981.

Banks, Leo W. and Craig Childs. *Grand Canyon Stories Then & Now*. Phoenix: Arizona Highways Books, 1999.

Butchart, J.H. "The Lower Gorge of the Little Colorado." *Arizona Highways Magazine* Sept. 1965: 34-42.

Butler, Elias. "Irresitible Lure, Inescapable Trap." *Arizona Daily Sun*. 18 January, 2002.

Carothers, Steven W. and Bryan Brown. *Colorado River Through Grand Canyon*. Tucson: University of Arizona Press, 1991.

Civil Aeronautics Board. *Accident Investigation Report*. 17 April, 1957.

Crumbo, Kim. *A River Runner's Guide to the History of the Grand Canyon*. Boulder, Colorado: Johnson Books, 1985.

Dolnick Edward. *Down the Great Unknown*. New York: Harper Collins Publishers, 2001.

Epple, Anne Orth. *Plants of Arizona*. Helena, Montana: Falcon Publishing,1995.

Evans, Edna. *Tales from the Grand Canyon: Some True, Some Tall*. Flagstaff, Arizona: Northland Press, 1976.

"Family Finds Discomfort Comforting." *Arizona Republic*. 2 July, 1956:3.

Fletcher, Colin. *The Complete Walker. New York*: Alfred A. Knopf,1981.

---. *The Man from the Cave*. New York: Alfred A. Knopf, 1981

---. *The Man Who Walked Through Time*. New York: Random House, 1968.

Ghiglieri, Michael P. *Canyon*. Tucson, Arizona: University of Arizona Press, 1992.

--- and Thomas M. Myers. *Over the Edge: Death in the Grand Canyon*. Flagstaff, Arizona: Puma Press, 2001.

Goldin, Greg. "Go Climb a Mountain, David Brower 1912-2000." *LA Weekly News*. Nov. 2000: 17-23.

Hendricks, Larry. "Missing Man Has History of Being Overdue." *Arizona Daily Sun*. 22 August, 2001.

Hornaday, William T. *Camp-Fires on Desert and Lava*. Tucson: University of Arizona Press, 1983.

Hughs, J. Donald. *The Story of Man at Grand Canyon.* Grand Canyon Natural History Association. Las Vegas: KC Publications, 1967.

Jeffers, Jo. "Tales of the Little Colorado." *Arizona Highways Magazine* Sept. 1965: 2-15.

Lofholm, Nancy. "News That 'Suicide' was Murder Odd Relief to Brother." *Denver Post.* 22 October, 2000.

Low, Sam. "Little Colorado Adventure Trek, From Baldy Mountain to the Sipapu." *Arizona Highways Magazine.* June 1983: 31-43.

MacMahon, James A. *Deserts.* New York: Alfred A. Knopf, 1985.

Myers, Tom, M.D. "The Waiting List" *The Newsletter of the Grand Canyon Private Boaters Association. Spring 2003.*

Page, Ted. "Memoir: The Accidental Guardian." *Boston Magazine.* April 2001.

Pirsig, Robert M. *Zen and the Art of Motorcycle Maintenance.* New York: William Morrow and Company, 1974.

Rivera, Jose de Jesus. "Spangler Pleads Guilty to Killing Wife in Grand Canyon." *Press Release.* Office of the United States Attorney District of Arizona. 27 December, 2000.

Robinson, Marilyn. "Deputy Plays Important Role in Solving Case." *Denver Post.* 6 October, 2000.

Rushoe, W. L. *Powell's Canyon Voyage.* Palmer Lake, Colorado: Filter Press, 1969.

Sadler, Crista. *There's This River*. Flagstaff, Arizona: This Earth Press, 2006.

Simmons, Leo W. *Sun Chief: The Autobiography of a Hopi Indian*. Clinton, Massachusetts: Yale University Press, 1942.

Spangler, Sharon. *On Foot in the Grand Canyon*. Boulder, Colorado: Pruett Publishing Company, 1989.

Thybony, Scott. *Burntwater*. Tucson, Arizona: University of Arizona Press, 1997.

Titiev, Mischa. "A Hopi Salt Expedition." *American Anthropolog*ist. Vol. 39 (1937): 244-258.

Wing, Kittridge and Lester Womack. "Bluewater Voyage in the Little Colorado River!" *Desert Magazine*. August, 1956

Wuerthner, George. *Grand Canyon, A Visitor's Companion*. Mechanicsburg, Pennsylvania: Stackpole Books, 1998.